THE LAWS OF
WISDOM

SHINE YOUR DIAMOND WITHIN

RYUHO OKAWA
IRH Press

Contents

Preface 17

Gift of Words for you
Information – Knowledge – Wisdom 18

⌒⌒ CHAPTER ONE ⌒⌒

The Grand Strategy for Prosperity

~ Each Person's Efforts and Perseverance
Open Up a Prosperous Future ~

1
For the Past Twenty-Eight Years,
I Have Taught What is Right

2
Big Government Always Leads to
The Corruption of a Nation

3
The Inner Revolution That is Needed Now

Return to the starting point and ask what you can do 28

Can you answer the question, "What is a human being?" ... 29

Now that the world population is headed for ten billion,
God is always watching over you 30

4
Filling the World with
The Breath of Prosperity Once Again

Having received commands from Heaven, think about
what you can do 32

What each person can do to create the Kingdom of God
on earth

  i) Be humble and explore the Right Mind 33

  ii) Each person needs to make their soul shine through
     perseverance and efforts 34

An independent person can protect the world from
dictatorship and tyranny 36

5
Right Wisdom Will Open
The Path to Prosperity 37

CHAPTER TWO

The Secrets of Intellectual Output

~ Ways of Studying and Working
That Produce Added Value ~

1
How is "Intellectual Output"
Different from "an Intellectual Life"?

Can you bring something of value to this world? 40

It is extremely difficult to have an intellectual life that
produces output 41

2
Learn from the Lifestyle of
The Philosopher Kant

Kant maintained a well-regulated lifestyle all his life 44

Intellectual output requires a certain amount of intellectual
reserves and "ripening" 47

Strong willpower and constant self-control are
necessary to form a habit 48

3
How to Live the 24 Hours in a Day
To the Full

Arnold Bennett advocated setting aside 90 minutes a day
for intellectual pursuits 49

Gathering trivial information from sources like newspapers
is a waste of time 50

How should you read newspapers? 52

4
Financial Freedom Enables
Intellectual Independence

People today have forgotten true intellectual joy 54

Private property is an extremely important "weapon" for
those who produce intellectual output 56

5
The Mental Attitude Required
To Create Intellectual Time

Break away from trivial socializing 60

You will not be capable of intellectual activities after
consuming alcohol 61

Make it a habit to include intellectual time in your
daily life 62

My intellectual life, and the reason I chose to work at a
trading company 63

Learning English was an added bonus from working at
the trading company 64

6
Work Techniques that Produce
Intellectual Output

Create your own area of specialization and explore it
in depth 67

The ideas of people with only one specialty are limited 68

Even if a subject is not your line of work, if you continue
to study it, you will become semi-professional 70

7
Acquiring a New Perspective
By Mastering a Foreign Language

You can get information that is unavailable in Japanese
from foreign language mass media 73

Do not be impatient to master a language; have the attitude
that you are sowing seeds in your garden 75

Ethnic and cultural differences apparent in Japanese and
English 77

8
Study History to Become an Educated Person

When you become a working adult you forget the history
you learned at school 79

If you do not know the history of your country you will
have a tough time overseas 81

9
Leading an Intellectual Life
That Enables You to Produce Intellectual Output

Innovation by uniting disparate elements 83

Amass information and "crystallize" it 85

In order to produce intellectual output, some kind of
gentle exercise is also necessary 86

CHAPTER THREE

The Power to Break Through Walls

~ The Power of the Mind
That Defeats Negative Thinking ~

1
The Negative Thinking
That Strongly Pervades Japan

Many people have the tendency to run into brick walls 90

The pattern of moving from "negative thinking" to
"thinking that maintains the status quo" 90

The importance of "the capacity to estimate," which can
be learned from swimming across rivers 92

Replace excuses for not being able to do things with
positive ideas 93

Why a bank-bashing drama, which showed how to break
through "impossible requirements," became popular in Japan ... 95

2
The Power to Think
That is Required of a Leader

Learning from the power to break through resistance and
survive, which works in the natural world 97

The power to think is the greatest weapon humans have ... 98

A leader must think ahead, not just focus on current tasks ... 100

3
Acquire Professional Skills

No one complains about how much a professional earns ... 102

Happy Science has gradually changed, becoming able
to work professionally 103

The Happy Science educational project is becoming
"professional" in a short time 104

4
I Want to Create Japanese Who
Break the Mold of the Typical Japanese

Building a school that can open up students' potential 107

Our role as an opinion leader to change common way of
thinking in Japan 108

An education that can produce people with the wish to
"enrich" the whole world 109

The resolution of builders to construct a temple that will
change the world 110

5
Aspirations Open Up a Path

The effects of education experienced through my English-
language teaching materials 112

English Vocabulary and Phrase Book goes beyond the level
of the "big three" private junior and senior high schools ... 114

Opening up a path with the greatest talent: The ability
to aspire 115

6
The Power of Management to Break Through Walls

The functions of management can be summed up as
marketing and innovation 118

It is a leader's mission to think constantly about working
effectively 120

CHAPTER FOUR

An Other-Dimensional Way of Thinking

~ How to Have Ideas that Transcend This World ~

1
What is an Other-Dimensional Idea?

People have different needs for an other-dimensional
way of thinking 124

The law of cause and effect is also at work when you
attract other-dimensional power 126

Power comes from other dimensions when preparations
in this world are complete 127

2
How to Get Other-Dimensional Ideas

1) Be someone who makes a habit of thinking 129

2) Acquire the seeds and materials for thinking 130

3) Continue to make worldly efforts 130

4) There is a difference between happiness and good luck 131

3
The Ryuho Okawa Style of
Other-Dimensional Thinking

The truth about Ryuho Okawa's writings, that is thought
to require a staff of at least 500 133

Simple efforts to receive other-dimensional power

    1) Make efforts to expand the scope of your interests 134

    2) Make efforts to expand your field of expertise 134

Make efforts to become a semi-professional in various fields ... 135

How to develop the capacity to receive sufficient spiritual
guidance from great composers 137

Sometimes narrow views of religion reject spiritual
guidance 137

As for a business owner, guiding spirits that match his
or her capacity will come 139

The anguish of a manga artist with a creative block 140

The second and later works of authors who write books
based on personal experiences are less interesting 141

Uninspired books based on documents are uninteresting 143

As well as just gathering and sorting information,
you also need to "crystallize" it 144

Allow the information you have gathered to ferment
and mature 145

You can acquire an international perspective by
studying languages 147

Intellectual training and faith are necessary to receive
spiritual messages 149

Keep firing "shells" with positive thinking 151

CHAPTER FIVE

Resourceful Leadership

~ Requirements for a Leader
Who Can Motivate Others ~

1
The Definition of a Leader in Various Situations

The meaning of "resourcefulness" in modern society 156

A leader is someone who knows what he or she has to do 157

What kind of person is a resourceful leader? 158

The risks for organizations that employ managers
incapable of making decisions 160

An ideal leader from the point of view of subordinates 162

2
An Organizational Culture
That Nurtures Leaders

Increase the number of people who can make decisions
within the organization 163

The high level of human resource training seen in
Starbucks part-timers 164

Strengthen the organization through human resource
training and boost profitability 166

3
The Resourcefulness and Efforts
Required to Establish Yourself
As a Professional

Without profit there is zero potential for growth 168

The costs of my lectures rose as the size of the venue
168increased 169

As a professional, I felt the pressure of taking money 171

Daily study is essential for a professional 172

The more the added value created by employees,
the bigger a company will grow 174

4
The Ability to Analyze Information
Required of a Leader

Strategies and tactics vary according to the leader's
judgment 176

The ability to discern what is right amongst information
that is publicly available 177

China's intentions can be picked up even from
newspaper articles 179

The company president also needs to restart his studies if
English is going to be the in-house official language 181

5
The Wisdom Needed to Expand Business

Requirements for motivating people:
1) Establish a noble purpose 184

Requirements for motivating people:
2) Being humble and having the attitude of making an effort 186

How to create employees like you and train management
staff 188

The reason why Happy Science makes it a priority to
solidify "software" into text 190

6
The Ability to Take Responsibility:
An Essential Quality for a Leader

The Ability to Take Responsibility:
An Essential Quality for a Leader 192

CHAPTER SIX

The Challenge of Wisdom

~ The Wisdom That Transcends Hatred and Saves the World ~

1
The Most Important Starting Point 196

2
The True Meaning of the "Right to Know"

What human beings truly need to know 198

There is a group of people shining brilliantly in the
midst of conflict and hatred 199

People today who are moving away from faith yield to
a materialistic civilization 200

Academic studies need the brighter light of wisdom 201

The power of wisdom distinguishes knowledge that
makes people happy from that which does not 202

3
In This Earthly World,
Give Others a Glimpse of Angelic Qualities

Attain wisdom that can save people, transcending the
differences and discrimination of this world 203

How to lead the people of your country to happiness
within a diversity of lifestyles 205

I wish to spread the Truth quickly, far and wide 206

Victory in this world and the mission of El Cantare 206

The work of the guiding spirits of Light on Earth 208

4
Under the Banner of Imperishable Truth

Wisdom is to attain the Truth universal to humanity 210

From "the challenge of entering the academic world"
to "the challenge of wisdom" 211

Afterword 213

About the Author 215

What Is El Cantare? 216

About Happy Science 218

Contact Information 220

Books by Ryuho Okawa 222

About HS Press 266

Preface

People are born into this world, live for a certain number of decades and eventually die. When they die, the only thing they can take back with them to the other world is their "mind." And within that mind what retains a diamond-like radiance is "wisdom."

In this book I have written from various angles about the wisdom that people need to acquire during their lifetime. I have presented many valuable thoughts, from how individuals should live their lives to the keys to intellectual output, as well as the secrets of management for business owners.

Modern-day enlightenment is something that is truly multi-faceted and complex. However, the most important thing is, through your own efforts, to shine a beam of light on your soul's way of life and to produce beautiful crystals in this precious lifetime.

I believe that, in a sense, I have successfully modernized the teachings of Buddha's Truth with the publication of *The Laws of Wisdom*, and last year's bestseller *The Laws of Perseverance*.

Ryuho Okawa
Founder and CEO of the Happy Science Group
December 2014

INFORMATION – KNOWLEDGE – WISDOM

"Information" is data
Which is constantly being collected
By your brain,
Through your eyes and ears.
"Information" can be
Accumulated or processed.

When "information" develops to the level
Where you can use it,
Or when it becomes academic ability
Or useful skills at work,
It serves as "knowledge."

"Knowledge" is power.
Possessing the knowledge that is necessary,
And being able to use it when needed
Is a vital skill and a weapon for surviving
In modern society.

However, there is something more important
Which is "wisdom."
When "knowledge" is deepened
Through experience,
And reaches a level where it can enrich
A person's views on life,
Serving as words of guidance for enlightenment,
That is called "wisdom."

"Wisdom" is born

When "knowledge" is filtered through good and evil.

It is crystallized

During deep reflection and meditation.

It closely resembles the inspiration

That comes down from one corner of Heaven.

Chapter One

The Grand Strategy for Prosperity

~ Each Person's Efforts and Perseverance
Open Up a Prosperous Future ~

Lecture given on July 8, 2014
at Saitama Super Arena
Saitama, Japan

1

For the Past Twenty-Eight Years, I Have Taught What is Right

The first time I stood in front of you and gave a lecture on a podium, awakening to the fact that this work was my mission, I was exactly thirty years old. It was ten years after I turned twenty, and I was giving a lecture commemorating the launch of Happy Science on November 23rd, 1986. During those ten years, my efforts and study had been accumulating continuously, and at the age of thirty, I stood firm, as Confucius said. Giving lectures on my own thoughts has become my life's work. I feel that the days go by very fast. Since that day, twenty-eight years have passed.

When I gave my very first lecture, people had gathered from all over Japan, but there were a total of only eighty-seven people. However, the lecture of this chapter, "The Grand Strategy for Prosperity," given on July 8th, 2014, on the occasion of the Celebration of the Lord's Descent, the lecture space, the Saitama Super Arena, was filled with people. It was also broadcast live to about 3,500 locations throughout Japan and around the world. My lectures have also been translated into over twenty-seven different languages, and published as books.

Slowly but surely, I feel that the Dharma Wheel is being turned and these teachings are spreading all over the world. This shows that the path I decided to take at the age of thirty and have walked continuously and wholeheartedly is a true path.

At the beginning, there were not so many people who believed in me. There were only a small number who believed the words of enlightenment sent from Heaven, what could be called the "revelation" that was bestowed on me.

However, the battle for Truth has been steadily moving forward, because I have continuously appealed to people's hearts. And the phrases I have always repeated are, "A fact is a fact, the truth is the truth" and "the Truth never dies."

Lies or falsity eventually perish as a result of various criticisms, accusations and attacks. However, the Truth always moves forward in the face of any criticism or headwind. I have shown, through my own life, how righteousness opens up a path in life and becomes a driving force to achieve greater progress.

2
Big Government Always Leads to The Corruption of a Nation

The title of this chapter is "The Grand Strategy for Prosperity." This is essentially a subject that the prime minister or president should speak about. However, if the lecture were for the whole world, maybe no one would be able to talk on this topic.

I, myself do not intend to give this talk on behalf of politicians. Rather, I want to tell you, from the standpoint of a religious leader, what kind of mindset you need to hold on to, and the basic attitude that is required of each one of you.

I feel that the current Japanese government is conducting a creative administration. We have not seen this kind of creative politics in Japan in the past, at the least in the past twenty years. Despite its frictions with other countries, Japan is currently producing a creative government, something rare for this country.

This being said, from the standpoint of religion, and also from the perspective of each person, we must think about politics in a different way. How, then, should we view it?

If, in fact, each citizen in the country has hopes of the great power of the government, expecting to receive aid, and if citizens think that by changing the system, the framework, or the structure of society, a brighter future will open up for them, you can say that something is lacking. From the standpoint of the soul training of each person, this sort of attitude is not enough.

Of course, I have no objection to the government engaging in excellent politics, with the appropriate national policies and strategies, and creating a brighter future. All the same, as citizens, we must never forget that big government will most likely lead people into corruption. This is something that history has proven.

It is dangerous to rely too much on the big powers. While we can receive the benefits that big government offers, each and every one of us living under this government must work on ourselves to grow as an independent person, who is able to make decisions and think about the future.

3

The Inner Revolution That is Needed Now

Return to the starting point and ask what you can do

"The Grand Strategy for Prosperity" is not something for the government alone to establish. The people who constitute the nation must also be involved. I am not just talking to Japan, but to people of nations around the world.

I am sure that in any country, the government does not function in a way that meets people's expectations. There is no government that fully meets the expectations of the people of a country. This is the reality.

However, you must understand that the outcome of government, in other words, the national strategy that those in the government are building, is the manifestation of the collective opinion of the citizens of that nation. If the individual quality of each citizen declines, the grand national strategy of a country, its politics, economy and various other structures will also become inadequate and unsatisfactory.

Therefore, I dare say to you: "Return to the starting point once again." I would like you to return to the starting point and think for yourself what *you* can do.

Can you answer the question, "What is a human being?"

I admit that the current Japanese government is doing well, though it is not perfect. However, one cannot just rely on the government and wait ten, twenty or thirty years for further improvement. The same can be said of other countries. Each and every citizen of a country needs to launch his or her own inner revolution.

What is this "inner revolution"? What is this "inner revolution" that is required of us now? What is this revolution that we are meant to start within our minds?

People living in this modern age of progressive scientific civilization continue to develop this civilization and this is a wonderful aspect of modern people. However, you have to be aware once again that you have forgotten something very, very important.

There are a lot of magnificent people in Japan as well, who have studied for ten or twenty years, have been to prestigious universities, and worked in good companies or gained various qualifications. Nonetheless, I cannot help but be astonished by the fact that these people do not even know the simple Truth. And there are many people being born now who think, "God is dead," "God doesn't exist anymore" or "Humans can take the place of God."

Certainly, if you compare this to 2,000 or 3,000 years ago, intellectuals nowadays seem to have knowledge and information that people back then were never able to have. To the eyes of people who lived long ago, it would probably seem as if we have a god-like wisdom.

Yet, if you cannot answer the questions, "What is a human being?" "Where were you before your birth, and where will you go after death?" "What is your objective in life?" then you can never be called a praiseworthy person. Rather, I have to say that all the knowledge, information and technology is clouding you, blocking you from seeing the truth.

Now that the world population is headed for ten billion, God is always watching over you

If God or Buddha existed 2,000 - 3,000 years ago, it is only natural to assume that He is watching over you now, in this present age when the population is increasing. There is no way that He is not.

When I started giving lectures, I gave messages to the five billion people in the world. But before I knew it, my messages were being sent to six billion people and now, I am addressing seven billion people in the world. The population of the Earth is increasing at a speed faster than the spread of my teachings.

It is tremendously difficult to bring an enormous global population that is heading for ten billion, prosperity and happiness, while maintaining peace. Do you really think God, Buddha, the Tathagatas, Bodhisattvas and Angels of Light in the heavenly world will remain indifferent to this challenge?

4
Filling the World with
The Breath of Prosperity Once Again

Having received commands from Heaven,
Think about what you can do

Right now, Japan is experiencing an affluent way of life, and so is America. Other countries are surely following them. In the world, however, more than one billion people are still suffering in poverty and hunger, and the numbers of these people will probably increase.

Even in Japan, more than twenty percent of the population is said to be living in poverty. The government is trying its best to come up with a plan to solve this problem now.

Nevertheless, do not just rely on the government. If you take the government for granted and depend on it, this country will sink in the course of time. Just as once prosperous countries have deteriorated, so this country will eventually head into decline.

Therefore transform your mind and rebuild it. Once again, fill the world on earth with the powerful breath of prosperity. That is what is important.

What then do you need to do now, in order to achieve that goal?

Heaven has already given us its commands. Heaven has already ordained for us, "Create the Kingdom of God on earth," "Create the Land of Buddha, a Buddhaland Utopia on earth." Those of you who believe these words must think about what you can do in response.

What each person can do to create The Kingdom of God on earth

i) Be humble and explore the Right Mind

The first thing I want to ask of you is to be humble. As human beings, people in this modern age know way more than those who lived in the past. Research is being undertaken in various fields, and has come as far as what is called "the domain of God." But you must know that, at the same time, people are also losing sight of something important.

It would be very sad if, by further study, people come to believe that the functioning of the human soul is merely the reaction of the brain, or the reaction of nerves. I am filled with deep sadness when I imagine that such people are now the leaders of this world.

Therefore, I want future leaders to be able to listen to the voice of Heaven open-heartedly and strive to realize Heaven's desires here on earth. To put it another way, this effort is to "explore the Right Mind," and "establish the Right Mind."

ii) Each person needs to make their soul shine Through perseverance and efforts

What you must do next is something truly ordinary and commonplace, something that has been spoken of for a long, long time. What is it?

It is the simple fact that, in order for humans to achieve success, become happy and prosper in this world, they need to persevere and make efforts. I want to confirm this very simple truth once again.

Throughout 2014, Happy Science has carried out activities based on my book, *The Laws of Perseverance* [New York: IRH Press, 2014]. I know this is an era when it is very difficult to move forward, even if you make consistent efforts. However, this time of perseverance definitely will not be a waste of your life. This time of perseverance is indeed a period when you are tested to see if you are the real deal.

People become successful not only because they have a high level of ability. Historically, many who succeeded did not have such superior abilities. Their abilities were not spectacular, but they persevered again and again, and never stopped making an effort. Such people overcame their difficulties one after another, and left behind giant steps in the history of humankind.

So please do not feel regret at not having enough ability or that you are not brimming with talent. In fact, this shows that expectations have been placed on you—for you to increase your soul's capacity and develop, in this lifetime, here on earth. It is also a chance for you.

If you think you have first-rate abilities, let me tell you that there have been many such people in the past. However, those who believe they have superior abilities tend to balk at making an effort. They rather think about getting through life as easily and efficiently as they can. They do not persevere, and in life they are easily distracted. They seek easy answers and wish for easy conclusions to come to them. In terms of faith, they ask for immediate results, for instance in the form of miracles.

But now, I tell you on behalf of all the guiding spirits in the heavenly world, that those in the heavenly world do not only wish for all your wishes to come true immediately. They wish from the bottom of their hearts for you to continue to persevere and make efforts through a number of decades in this world. They wish for you to build on your achievements and walk the path to success, while continuing to refine your soul.

An independent person can protect the world
From dictatorship and tyranny

The heavenly beings are right beside you, giving you advice on which direction you should go in. Nonetheless, it is the duty and the right of each and every person to actually make efforts while persevering, and to achieve success while wishing for the happiness of others.

Instead of wanting to be given everything, I hope that you will live a life sharing with others your happiness at having being born into this world, even if it is through small acts.

On a global scale, there are major issues. There are issues involving war and peace, and also issues involving the relationship between peace and prosperity. These are all big, big issues that a single individual cannot deal with. However, what we must be careful about now is this: we must prevent a dictator or tyrant from emerging and leading many people in the wrong direction, in a world with a population headed toward seven billion.

In order to do this, as I have just said, effort, discipline, and perseverance, as well as an attitude of continually learning, are required on the part of each and every person who is independent. A country that has produced a lot of these sorts of people will protect the world.

5
Right Wisdom Will Open The Path to Prosperity

Have right awareness. Have the wisdom to tell good from evil.

We must produce such people, otherwise we cannot lead the world in the right direction.

We must create many such people, otherwise we cannot open the path to prosperity.

Right now, it is not possible for just one person to make the world happy. While I can give each and every person advice, happiness is something that each person must grasp with his or her own hands. Please do not forget this.

Do not rely on big government. Rather, every one of you must raise your individual quality as a human. And your cooperative power, in networks and groups, will create a great flow, improving the country and making the country prosperous and peaceful.

Should an ambitious country rise up, it is important to teach its people properly what the right way is. If you, yourself are practicing this, you can teach it to others.

Any abuse and criticism thrown at people who have a peaceful mind and live every day persevering and making efforts will be reflected back at those who fired those words.

This is how the Truth works.

The Truth is a mirror. The one in the mirror is not someone else. It is you, yourself, and your own country.

Be righteous!
The righteous must be strong,
The righteous must be good,
The righteous must prosper.
Build a peaceful future in the midst of prosperity.

I have high hopes for you.
Let us work together and construct a new "future age."

Chapter Two

The Secrets of Intellectual Output

~ Ways of Studying and Working
That Produce Added Value ~

Lecture given on December 31, 2011
at Sacred Shrine of Great Enlightenment, Taigokan
Tokyo, Japan

1
How is "Intellectual Output" Different from "an Intellectual Life"?

Can you bring something of value to this world?

In 2010 alone, I gave a total of 229 lectures. The following year I did not need to give any election campaign speeches to support the Happiness Realization Party, so there were slightly fewer but still, in 2011, I gave 216 lectures. Since then I have given a similar number of lectures and published many books each year, so I continue to produce intellectual output in this way. [As of the end of December 2014, the number of books published reached 1800.]

The theme of this chapter is "The Secrets of Intellectual Output," which I believe to be an extremely important topic. There is so much to say about this topic that it would probably take two or three books. However, revealing everything in one fell swoop would spoil your pleasure, so on this occasion I have decided to limit my discourse to just one chapter. But in the past I have woven strands of similar themes through my talks.

Intellectual output is very important to someone like me who gives various lectures and sermons throughout the year, publishes many books, works while deepening different ideas and in addition, runs a religious organization.

An intellectual life is possible if you carve out time to read books and study various topics, but when it comes to intellectual output that alone is not enough. For intellectual output, you have to produce something and in that sense, you need to be productive. In other words, you have to bring something of value into this world, you have to produce some added value.

If you are satisfied just to study, you have not reached a level of intellectual output. Cramming for exams does count as studying, but it is only about getting a certain score in a test, so you can hardly say that you are producing something. You are probably "confirming" your intellectual ability but you are not yet going as far as to "produce" something intellectual. If you are the one creating the test questions, you could then perhaps say that you are in the position of producing an intellectual output though it may be small.

It is extremely difficult to have
An intellectual life that produces output

There is a difference between compulsory study, or "study that you are made to do passively," and "study to produce output," which is based on the active way of life that accompanies productivity.

It is, of course, impossible to say definitively which one is of greater value, but the latter "an active intellectual life" or "an intellectual life that produces output" is the life of someone who is regarded as a "professional," and the reality is that it involves a greater level of difficulty. Nevertheless, it is impossible to say which brings a greater sense of happiness.

I imagine that it would probably be nice to spend my days reading the classics after retiring, without writing books or giving any talks, like a highly intellectual elderly gentleman. Ever since I was young, I have somehow been attracted to that kind of lifestyle. However, my situation does not allow me to lead such a lifestyle; I have to give the fruits of my study back to society. Increasingly I find myself in a situation where I am not allowed to keep my studies just for myself.

As long as you study just for the sake of your own job or your own life, you do not have so much responsibility. However, if you continuously study and have reached a level where your intellectual satisfaction should be made of service to many people, your studies then need to be transformed into something for the public. And you need to express your ideas or announce your opinions to the public in some way.

This can be done at various levels, from novice to professional. Some special skills need to be added, beyond mere "methods of study."

There are plenty of people in this world who read books and gather information. You can also pick up information by watching TV or looking at the Internet, just as you can get information from a mobile phone or some other means. However, if you simply receive information passively, it is mere consumption, and it is the same as just listening to what someone has to say.

On the other hand, when it comes to making that information your own, reworking it and condensing it to produce your own ideas, you will need to have sufficient skills and experience, as well as a kind of wisdom.

2
Learn from the Lifestyle of The Philosopher Kant

Kant maintained a well-regulated lifestyle all his life

At the start of this chapter I spoke about the number of lectures I have given. Actually, a few days ago I dipped into a book of philosophy by Immanuel Kant and was stunned when I read that there were periods in his life when Kant gave 20 lectures a week.

The content of his lectures is rather difficult, so I have to say that I was amazed that he could deliver such difficult lectures 20 times a week. I am not sure if he took long breaks between such periods, but if he lectured 20 times a week without taking breaks that would mean a thousand lectures a year, which would be a great and arduous endeavor.

If he delivered 1,000 lectures a year, given that he lived a long life [Kant died at the age of 79] he would have produced a tremendous amount of intellectual output. However, he did not produce that much, so I guess that to some extent the figure includes repeat lectures to students.

Kant led a lifestyle that is very difficult to outdo. For example, it is well known that he was an early riser who got up at 5 o'clock in the morning. Winter or summer, he would get up at 5 a.m. and breakfast on just a cup of tea. A heavy meal dulls intellectual thinking, so he would have some tea and then start his work or studies. He would spend around two hours studying or planning his lectures, and then from 7 a.m. he would give classes in his home.

I often preach at *Taigokan*, the Sacred Shrine of Great Enlightenment, so there is a parallel with his lifestyle. Kant did not go to the university to give classes but instead taught in his own home from 7 a.m. He gave classes that lasted roughly an hour or longer, between around 7 and 8 o'clock, with the students coming to his house. He maintained that pattern for a long time.

Kant employed an elderly chamberlain, a kind of manservant, who woke him before 5 a.m. Kant did not like to wake up straightaway, so the manservant would frantically awake him because Kant would get very angry with him if he did not.

Kant would get up at 5 a.m. and then spend two hours studying or preparing his lectures, or sometimes writing, before giving his early morning class. If, after completing his duties as a university professor, he still had the energy, he would then write until lunchtime.

He would invite friends capable of intellectual conversation for lunch, and would spend rather a long time, about three hours, taking his midday meal.

Apparently there was sometimes wine. Then, at the same time every afternoon, he would take up his stick and go out for a walk.

This is the life that Kant led in the German country town of Königsberg, and it is said that he never left his hometown, not even once. It truly is amazing, but he never went on any trips or left Königsberg, instead living surrounded by books and only going out for walks. It was probably because going on a trip would disturb the regular routine of his life and, on top of that, he would not be able to take his books with him.

So Kant woke up at 5 o'clock every morning and he also went out for walk at a set time every day. There is even a story that shows how punctual he was, which is that his neighbors would set their clocks on seeing him setting out for his afternoon walk.

Apparently he usually did not bother with an evening meal, so he was probably close to a lifestyle of "one meal a day." He may sometimes have taken a light meal, but he got most of his nutrition from his substantial lunch, to which he would invite various people and enjoy intellectual conversations.

In the evening he would study, turn the lights out at 10 p.m. and wake up at 5 a.m. Apparently Kant repeated this pattern day after day.

Intellectual output requires a certain amount of Intellectual reserves and "ripening"

Kant did not write all that many books when he was young, but from his late fifties he started to produce books in quick succession and in his fifties and sixties he published many great works. This really is an unusual case. Generally speaking, people start writing books when they are a little younger and gradually, as they get older, they become less able to write. However, in Kant's case, he produced a string of great works at a more advanced age.

The reason behind this lies in his lifestyle, leading a well-regulated life and the continual process of building up his intellectual reserves. In the field of humanities in particular, intellectual reserves are extremely important. You need to build up a certain level of intellect, as well as allowing the intellect to mature, just like a fine cheese. You cannot produce anything particularly noteworthy simply by relaying unprocessed information to others.

If you leave what you have learned to ferment and mature, some of it will turn into wisdom. As you continue to study, you will find that some of the things you have learned are worthless, junk knowledge, and some of it remains as gold dust. So, as you continue devoting time to your studies, you gradually need to sift out the gold dust and make an effort to combine all this gold dust and create a gold nugget, or something like an engraving of a goldsmith. That is actually what Kant did.

Strong willpower and constant self-control Are necessary to form a habit

I imagine that there are not many people today who are capable of emulating Kant's lifestyle, but there are certainly several points to be learnt from his way of life. One thing that can be said is that it is difficult to continue to produce intellectual output unless you have successfully made it a habit to lead an intellectual life.

I know this because in the past for more than five years I had a corporate life. When you work for a company, there are a lot of irregular hours, and it often happens that you lose your freedom with regard to your time and lifestyle. On the worldly level, there is not only working overtime but also an obligation to socialize. You feel obligated to go for a drink or sing *karaoke*. Sometimes I was summoned to join others on my day off and go to places like clubs. This type of socializing can be very taxing.

It is thus very difficult to establish your own habits to the extent where you are able to produce intellectual output. It requires strong willpower and constant self-control until you have firmly established these habits.

3
How to Live the 24 Hours in a Day
To the Full

Arnold Bennett advocated setting aside
90 minutes a day for intellectual pursuits

Most people may find it rather difficult to emulate Kant. In that case, it is important to focus on setting aside some time each day.

A British author who lived around a century ago, Arnold Bennett [1867 – 1931], spoke about this. He said that whether or not you are living the 24 hours a day to the full is determined by how you spend each day.

I learned quite a lot from his thinking. If I were to summarize his assertion, it would be to make sure to put aside 90 minutes a day. Bennett says that since there are a lot of things going on it may be difficult to practice, but somehow you have to carve out about 90 minutes a day for intellectual pursuits.

This applies in the case of working adults; in the case of people who can study all day long, like students, it is slightly different. What Bennett is saying is something along the lines of "If you can put aside 90 minutes a day, after a few years this will produce a huge effect. If you spend 90 minutes a day on some particular area of study, after a few years, let's say after three years, you will have become an expert on it." However, it requires considerable effort and self-discipline to set aside those 90 minutes.

Gathering trivial information from sources Like newspapers is a waste of time

Bennett observed the citizens of London, and saw company workers riding the packed commuter trains in the morning. In order to reach their office as soon as they could, they would try to ride as near to the front of the train as possible, cramming themselves into the carriages. And most of them read nothing but the newspaper.

There are thus many people who read the newspaper in the morning, but newspapers are actually nothing but "a pile of corpses." All sorts of things are written in newspapers about events that have happened the previous day, but the information they contain is of the sort that will be tossed away in the evening and no one will have bothered to read it by that time. Nevertheless, people read the newspaper avidly.

They use their time on the train, an hour or maybe more, to read newspapers, then head to the office with a weary brain and reluctantly start work. That is what they do. Bennett issued the warning against these newspapers more than a century ago.

Nowadays there is even more that people need to be warned of. After the newspaper, the radio and then the TV became popular. These days, a lot of trivial information reaches us from various sources, such as mobile phones and the Internet.

Some of it is useful information, but the majority of it rather wastes your time, so you have to be courageous and make an effort to sort out the data that is useful. And you must think about how to put aside around 90 minutes a day, just an hour and a half.

Bennett says that if you simply cannot get out of socializing and cannot put aside those 90 minutes on weekdays, you have to steel yourself and make up for that on your days off. I have had the experience of working at a trading company so I really do understand what he is saying.

Most trading company employees are highly educated and, of course, many of them are competent in English when they join the company. However, once they have joined the company there is a tendency for their intellectual level to steadily decline because of all the time they spend socializing. They become unable to read difficult or detailed books unless they have a great deal of persistence or strong will.

Even the so-called "elite" who graduated from the University of Tokyo and have lived overseas for a long time generally tend to read only a couple of mystery novels a month on average, in addition to things like weekly magazines and, objectively speaking, they can no longer be said to be intellectual.

How could it be otherwise? They are so busy that their brains become numb so they can no longer read anything heavy and only want to read things that are light and insubstantial. Probably their only intellectual stimulation comes from reading the newspaper.

How should you read newspapers?

Having said this, we should not take newspapers lightly. It takes a fair amount of time to read a newspaper thoroughly, and it is said that a newspaper generally contains about the same amount of information as two paperbacks. The important thing here is to know that you do not need all the information contained in a newspaper.

Of course your brain finds it very tiring to read the equivalent of two paperbacks' worth of information in a morning, so if you read the entire newspaper with the same level of attention it is true to say that you will use up a fair bit of your reserves of energy for the day's work. To prevent that happening, it is important to select the sections of the newspaper that hold the information you need and read those thoroughly, and just get a rough impression of everything else.

Things like weekly magazines can of course be an important source of information, and when it comes to current affairs there is information that you can only get from weekly magazines. But with these too, you should just read the parts with important information and not spend too much time on the rest.

More than a century ago Bennett advised us that reading the newspaper in the morning will leave you exhausted, and I was well aware of that fact. But of course I do still read newspapers. Bennett himself admitted that he too read several papers a day, but apparently he avoided doing so in the morning. Perhaps he read them in the afternoon. News inevitably tends to be a lot of bad news, so it is often the case that it is tiring to read.

4

Financial Freedom Enables
Intellectual Independence

People today have forgotten true intellectual joy

The Internet culture is flourishing now and many people use the Internet to obtain information. It is easy to look things up so it is a source of all kinds of data. This is also an age in which even ordinary people can transmit information, so the number of writers and readers is increasing.

In that sense, the Internet is advancing the "popularizing of a knowledge-based society" or the "democratization of knowledge." While this is a good thing, it cannot be denied that when it comes to studying things in depth to an expert level, there is a tendency for a slight dumbing-down. This is due to the choice of information and knowledge. Furthermore, the threat of the imminent disappearance of paper books is a trend today, and it is often said that soon everyone will read only electronic books, not paper ones.

This democratization of knowledge is good in the sense that many people will have easy access to books and will be able to acquire various kinds of knowledge. On the other hand, however, it may also be true to say that the number of people who do not know true intellectual joy and fulfilment will increase. After all, people in the past were able to experience a kind of joy that even we are unable to experience today.

When it comes to books, as much as possible I collect well-bound books because reading such books makes me feel rich. Since tatty books often do not stand up to repeated readings, I buy well-bound books as often as I can and I intend to read them again in my old age. But even so, I still only get a low level of joy from them.

In the past books had sealed pages and people had to cut the pages open with a paper knife to read them. That must have been a source of great pleasure. It is something we cannot experience today. It must have felt really good to cut open the pages one at a time as you read them.

If a book was serious there must have been an intense joy in knowing that you were the very first person to cut open that page and read it. It is a great shame that no one today can experience that kind of sophisticated delight, not even me.

Today we have sealed pages only on weekly magazines and tabloids. Apparently the pages with lewd contents are sealed, and you cannot see what is inside unless you rip open the pages. I am not talking about that kind of thing here but about serious books; it must have been a truly refined pleasure to cut open the pages of a serious book one at a time and then read them.

I presume that it was one of the pleasures of aristocrats who owned mansions and had well-stocked libraries. In those times the number of intellectuals was also fairly small. Nowadays we are no longer able to experience that pleasure.

Private property is an extremely important "weapon" For those who produce intellectual output

What I am trying to say here is this: it is a good thing that there is progress in the democratization of knowledge, that our world has become very convenient and that now there are many people above a certain intellectual level. Unfortunately, however, to be able to produce intellectual output in today's world, you need to have a certain amount of private property at your disposal.

But in the olden days people often practiced the exact opposite. For example, Indian philosophy includes some works that were just learnt by ear; people would listen to teachings passed down by word of mouth and memorize them all. Ancient philosophical treatises such as *The Upanishads* were all from an oral tradition passed on by word of mouth and learned by rote.

Such traditions do exist, but nowadays if you want to progress from being someone who leads an intellectual life to become someone who produces intellectual output, to a certain extent you need to have assets at your disposal. In that sense, private property is an extremely important "weapon" for someone who produces intellectual output.

If you want to protect your intellectual life, you must be wary of ideologies such as socialism and communism that do not permit private assets. Under such ideologies, people will ultimately be put in a situation where they cannot obtain any knowledge or information. While the communist party elite alone can issue guiding principles, everyone else must be satisfied just to read them. Or, as in the China of old, they are reduced to a level where everyone has a copy of the red book, *Quotations from Chairman Mao Tse-Tung*, and can read only that. If that is acceptable to you, you could hold to a belief system that does not allow private assets.

However, to secure circumstances where you can study freely without feeling constrained, without being suppressed by anyone, financial freedom is necessary as the foundation. After all, it is important to have a certain amount of private assets available to ensure intellectual freedom. If they are taken away, intellectual life becomes very difficult.

In the past, aristocrats in foreign countries had huge mansions. As we often see in movies, British aristocrats owned huge estates, which as the landowners they inherited. An intellectual class could continue to exist in such countries because they could pass on their assets undiminished to their heirs.

In Japan however, due to the tax system, the money earned by someone who has successfully built a fortune will be reduced to zero after three generations. His fortune will be completely taken by tax.

A typical example of this was the family of Michiko Shoda, who became the empress consort of Japan. The area called Ikedayama in Tokyo used to have the assurance of an upper-class residential area based on the fact that the Shoda residence was located there, but when the father of Her Majesty the Empress died, her siblings had to hand over the family home to pay the inheritance tax.

I believe that Her Majesty's elder brother worked for the Bank of Japan and her younger brother became president of Nisshin Flour Milling Company after working for the Industrial Bank of Japan. Even though they were people of considerable wealth, because they could not pay the inheritance taxes, they had to pay in kind with real estate.

The family home of Her Majesty the Empress was demolished after it had been used to pay off the taxes, and the site is now a small and uninteresting park. It is not large enough to give children much room to play. In fact, I wonder about the benefits of the park as the maintenance costs alone are probably quite substantial.

In that sense, basically I do not agree very much with philosophies that suppress the financial freedom of individuals, and lead to the taking away of intellectual freedom. This is because I believe that it is a path that leads to people becoming enslaved. In the past the idea of honest poverty may have been fine, but nowadays we need a certain degree of intellectual independence.

5

The Mental Attitude Required To Create Intellectual Time

Break away from trivial socializing

Company employees have difficulty in producing intellectual output, and the reason for this is that a company is a kind of "village" which they cannot leave. If they act differently from others, they will inevitably end up as a target of negative criticism, such as being labelled unsociable. So it can be difficult for employees to escape their social obligations.

However, if you want to engage in activities that involve intellectual output, you simply have to let go of social obligations. I realized this at a comparatively young age.

Some events are simply unavoidable and you have to resign yourself to those things. However, on occasions other than those, you need to absent yourself from social obligations when possible, otherwise you will be unable to make time for yourself. By nature I myself am sociable, but I started to avoid my social duties fairly consistently and have made it a rule not to do anything that wastes my time. In that sense, I may have seemed to be slightly unsociable.

As I mentioned earlier, Arnold Bennett tells people like salaried workers to put aside 90 minutes a day, but this is impossible to do unless you make a real effort. There are some social occasions that you simply cannot refuse to attend, but there are also some you could do without. You have to break away from the kind of socializing that is just meeting up because people have nothing else to do. It is important to break away from trivial socializing as much as you can.

You will not be capable of intellectual activities After consuming alcohol

It is not that I cannot drink alcohol, but basically I have stopped drinking. In my case, I stopped drinking because after I have a drink I become incapable of intellectual activities. I think it is fine to have a drink and have a great time if that is the end of your day's activities and afterwards you can simply go to sleep. I think it is fine for people like factory workers to wind down with a drink at the end of the day and then go to sleep.

However, it would be very difficult to study or write at home if you have had a drink after work. It is basically impossible. After you have had a drink it is hard to concentrate, so you cannot read a book, and there is no way that you could do something like write a manuscript. That is why I no longer drink much alcohol.

Make it a habit to include intellectual time In your daily life

It is very hard to create the time for intellectual pursuits. People who lead an eccentric kind of lifestyle like Kant's have a bit more freedom with their time. A university professor, too, can lead a life relatively close to that of someone self-employed, so even if he spends his time in a different way from other people, probably nobody will say anything.

To a certain extent, you have to make it a habit to include intellectual time. To do this you have to factor into your daily life ways to create time for study, and ways to create time to produce intellectual output. This is the basic attitude required of you.

Someone who cannot make a habit of this is, unfortunately, not capable of producing intellectual output. There are some authors who, when they are young, force themselves to stay up all night writing, trying really hard to meet deadlines, but they often tend to self-destruct at some point and have a short career. They tend to over-abuse their brain or stamina, and in time they wear themselves out.

When you display intense concentration, or undergo intense stress, your character will disintegrate in reaction to this unless you make sure you have some time for recreation. After all, people who are always pursuing deadlines, people who shut themselves away from the world to concentrate on writing, in a sense may unfortunately not be very intellectual. It is very tough to shut yourself away to write countless episodes of a serial, but it will not make you intellectual.

My intellectual life, and the reason I chose to work At a trading company

It is a blessing to be on a sound financial footing if you want to secure a certain degree of intellectual independence. With a secure financial footing there will be less risk of being subject to communist or socialist restraints and, at the same time, you do not have to read or write about things you do not like. In other words, you have the flexibility that allows you to focus on the things you are interested in.

Relatively few people comment on financial assets, but this attitude is important. I believe that it is a good thing to have a regular income.

As I have explained several times before, I chose to work for a trading company for the following reasons. In those days not many companies had a five-day week. It was an era when most companies worked six days a week, but trading companies had already adopted a five-day working week and paid a comparatively high salary.

Furthermore, I was assigned to the administrative

division, the financial affairs department that dealt with the banks. Banks close their doors at 3 p.m. so there is not much coming and going after that. On top of that, the employees of banks do not make many demands on their clients for pointless socializing.

So I chose that job in order to secure time for studying and a source of income. Looking back at the years I worked there, I think that, to a certain extent, the job served these purposes well.

Learning English was an added bonus
From working at the trading company

Perhaps an additional benefit of working at a trading company was the linguistic competence I acquired. It was an added bonus that I needed to study English for my work and so that is how I improved my English.

While working at the trading company it is possible to study English during working hours, not just after going home. Some sections use English all day; they write all their documents and hold their conversations in English. Reading books in English is rather tough, but I was reading documents in English all day at work so I was reading a considerable amount of English. I do not know how many books all the documents would be equal to if added up. I certainly read a huge amount of English print.

I also wrote letters in English, and had to write in a style appropriate for contracts. I would type out and send letters, so it is true to say that in the course of my work I naturally acquired the ability to read and write English.

However, that alone was not enough. It was a world where unless you had done further study, you would naturally lose out to your rivals.

While it was a little unexpected, I needed English more than I had thought and as a result my linguistic skills were honed. I had been born and raised in the countryside and neither of my parents was good at English, they could not speak English at all. My home was not the kind of intellectual environment where foreign languages such as English were used. But I became able to use English mainly because of my work environment.

As a result I can now work in English; I am capable of producing intellectual output related to English, for example publishing English books and textbooks, and I can even give lectures in English. This was an unexpected by-product, and one for which I am grateful.

When your work actually has a certain degree of relevance to an intellectual life like this, there will be more added value. But generally speaking, most jobs do not have much of a connection to that.

Although paperwork is good for training the brain at the beginning, as you continue to do it for a long time it will no longer be such an intellectual task. Nevertheless, there are plenty of people who believe that these types of jobs offer their brain far more training than being a housewife.

6
Work Techniques that Produce Intellectual Output

Create your own area of specialization And explore it in depth

Another thing I want to talk about in this chapter is work methods. In fact, there are work methods that assist the production of intellectual output. So, what are they?

Of course, it is important to take an interest in things because you cannot do things that you have no interest in. However, you cannot attain inner stability unless you have some kind of specialization. Therefore, you need to explore some particular area in depth until you feel that you have, to some extent, reached the level of an expert. Unless you delve as deeply as that, even though you may sample a number of different areas and know about many different things, you will only be "a trivia expert" and not an "intellectual expert."

Today, people who are expert at processing trivia often become famous in the mass media, but such people are not intellectuals in the true sense of the word.

Truly profound self-confidence will not emerge unless you possess some form of specialization, so it is important there is some area you have delved deeply into so that you have the confidence to be able to say that you are an expert in it to some extent. While having this expertise, it is important to expand out from it, little by little, into other fields that you find interesting. You should cultivate these other interests gradually, just as you would flowers. You have to nourish them with fertilizer, water them, give them sunlight and let them grow, little by little.

Rather than thinking, "I'll cut the flowers now and put them in a vase" or "I'll harvest them now and eat them," you gradually need to cultivate areas in which you have an interest until you reach a semi-professional level, if not the level of an expert. This process relates to my next point about how to come up with different ideas.

The ideas of people
With only one specialty are limited

People who have only one specialty become unable to see from any other perspective. They become incapable of producing any ideas that would appeal to others. This is one of the reasons that "intelligent" people end up becoming inept workers.

In the humanities, for example, there are many brilliant people in the law department and they become very good at matters pertaining to the law. However, the more brilliant they are, the more incompetent they are when they are given ordinary work to do. They see everything in a legalistic way and are not able to do any other work.

I know that top judges, lawyers and public prosecutors are intelligent, but as to whether you can employ them in a company and make good use of them, the answer is you cannot. They are not fit for any other work, so they cannot be utilized in any areas other than their specialty. They might be able to do things like investigations for the Legal Department, but nothing else. This is one of the risks of having only one area of expertise: an expert's way of looking at things becomes fixed.

There are very few lawyers who can write a lot of books. The same goes for judges and public prosecutors. They get very fixed in their ideas. The same may be true of doctors as well. There have always been people who are doctors and novelists at the same time, but generally speaking they are sloppy doctors [*laughs*].

Being a doctor provides a certain level of income and it is a life-long profession from which you cannot be fired, so it is possible to accumulate assets to maintain intellectual independence. For this reason, in any era there have always been doctors who would try and write books in their spare time, using their assets as a lever to create stability. However, if they are highly capable doctors, they will not be able to write that much either. They might be able to write specialized medical papers, but when it comes to anything else they are not much use.

Nowadays the tendency is for those who are talented to specialize, so such doctors become incapable of dealing with the entire body and most likely end up as specialists in something. Of course that in itself serves a useful role, so if you are satisfied just to make a living and get ahead in your field of specialization, then that is perfectly fine.

Even if a subject is not your line of work,
If you continue to study it,
You will become semi-professional

If you want to present your own ideas to be read by different kinds of people, and to go as far as inspiring people intellectually, simply studying your own area of specialization is not enough.

Suppose you are a lawyer who also has an interest in reading literature, for instance novels. If you go beyond a certain level in reading novels, it is possible that you may become a literary connoisseur. Or, if your hobby is watching movies, it is possible that you will watch all sorts of movies just like a movie critic.

It may also be the case that you are interested in economics and while being a lawyer you continuously study a number of different topics connected with economics. Or you may have specialized in law in the law department of university but also be interested in politics and, after graduating, continue to study politics.

These are examples of areas of study other than your own area of specialization. If you continue doing a certain amount of study in these areas, you will gradually become semi-professional. Also you will be able to see things from a different perspective.

Usually a legal specialist can only express legal opinions; he cannot say anything else. But if he is interested in literature and has read many novels, he will also be able to talk about more general subjects and say things like, "This is my opinion as a legal expert, but in a case such as this there are also various other opinions in the world at large." This sort of person has transcended the framework of a lawyer and so has the potential to become an author whilst also making use of the law.

Lawyers like this who can also read novels are rare, but if they also understand economics and become lawyers who can write from the economic angle as well, that will give them another perspective. And if they also become capable of talking about politics, their field of expertise will gradually expand.

So what happens when a practicing lawyer also progresses in his studies of subjects like economics and politics? There are many cases where people from the legal profession become politicians, and generally speaking these people have been interested in other fields and have done a certain amount of studying. If they had not, it would be very difficult for them to turn into politicians. Of course, they may not go beyond a certain level as lawyers and at a certain point they have to stop pursuing expert knowledge in fields other than their own, but it may be possible for them to attain success in other fields.

There are not many politicians who write books. There may be some who publish a book by using a ghost writer before becoming prime minister. That is probably the best they can do.

Nonetheless, we can say that politics is an extremely creative profession in the sense that politicians need to think about and create new things. We can say that mapping out a country's path and structure is a kind of creation. In order to do that kind of creative work, it is important to have multiple perspectives. Please be aware of this.

7
Acquiring a New Perspective
By Mastering a Foreign Language

***You can get information that is unavailable
In Japanese from foreign language mass media***

In the first part of this chapter I spoke about English. Language is actually an extremely big issue, particularly nowadays.

More than 120 million inhabitants of Japan speak Japanese, but there really are very few people in other countries who speak Japanese. Overseas, Japanese can only be understood by those who have studied it at university or lived in Japan, so there is practically no prospect of Japanese becoming an official language of the United Nations. Since that is the case, I would also like to recommend mastering other languages.

To master a foreign language takes an extremely long time, but once you have achieved a certain degree of mastery you can see things from a new perspective. There is huge intellectual merit in the sense that you become able to acquire information that is not available in your own language.

I always watch CNN in the morning. The regions from which CNN reports come are mostly ones where the Japanese newspapers and TV channels have not stationed any correspondents. The CNN correspondents are constantly reporting from places where shells are whizzing through the air, buildings are going up in flames and tanks are rumbling by.

Japanese journalists do not want to risk their lives, so they usually do not go to such places. All they do is post articles that have been edited and derived from reports written in other countries. So if you can watch and understand CNN, it is a huge advantage in the sense that you can get to know about events you would otherwise not be aware of, if you were simply reading the articles in Japanese. That is one of the benefits of competency in a foreign language.

In 2003 there was the Iraq War, and before that the Gulf War in 1990 and 1991, and at that time even the Iraqi leader Saddam Hussein watched CNN intently. Apparently Saddam Hussein watched CNN because he did not know where was being attacked unless he watched CNN. He did not know which places were under attack from the information provided by his own army. That is what I heard.

It is true to say that mastering a world language to a level where you can use it is an advantage both for transmitting and acquiring information. It is no use unless you reach a certain level of proficiency, but once you get as far as the level where you can actually use it, it offers tremendous merits.

There is a lot of merit in being able to read foreign language newspapers and watch foreign language TV. Being able to read books in foreign languages will also bring many benefits.

Do not be impatient to master a language; Have the attitude that you are sowing seeds In your garden

In mastering a language, you must not be impatient. It is true that there are some people with a talent for mastering languages in a very short time, but sometimes people who pick them up quickly have only a superficial understanding. There are also quite a lot of people who quickly become able to hold a conversation but do not get any further than that. So I do not want you to lament too much if you are slow to master a foreign language.

Mastering a foreign language is like farming; you have to keep on studying, telling yourself that this will not bear fruit immediately.

In 2011, I gave lectures in English in seven places in Asia [India, Nepal, the Philippines, Hong Kong, Singapore, Malaysia and Sri Lanka]. Of course I have not skipped a day of my English studies, but looking back at 2011, I studied a number of other languages besides English.

I went to India first so I studied Hindi as well. Since I went to Mumbai in addition to Delhi, I also studied a little Tamil and Marathi because these are the languages used in Mumbai.

When I gave my lecture in English in Singapore, a Q&A session was also scheduled. People in Singapore speak "Singlish," which is English spoken with a Chinese accent, so there was a rather strong possibility that I would not be able to understand the questioners' English. In order to be able catch what they are saying, you need to be able to understand Chinese, and in particular Chinese spoken with a southern accent.

I had studied this when I went to lecture in Taiwan in 2008. Studying the Chinese of the south a bit acquainted me with the pronunciation of the Chinese words, and it trained me to pick up on the accent. I studied it so as to be able to anticipate how English would change when overlaid with that accent.

Even if you cannot actually master it, if you study even a little the pronunciation of southern Chinese languages such as Cantonese, when you hear English spoken with that accent you can imagine how the original English would be if you took away the accent, and you get a rough idea of what is being said even if there is a strong accent. That is what I did.

I also studied Thai a little though I could not go to Thailand due to the flooding. I also studied Malay for my trip to Malaysia, and finally Sinhalese, the language spoken by 70% of the population, for my visit to Sri Lanka. I read several textbooks about each language.

However, I resigned myself to not getting as far as mastery of those languages. That is because I know that it is no easy thing to master a language.

In fact it takes years to master a language and it is not something that can be done quickly. What I did was simply sowing seeds to begin with. It may indeed be only at the level of tilling the soil and sowing seeds, but to some extent I study the language of the places I visit. Sooner or later the ones for which I have an aptitude will probably start to bear fruit little by little. Nevertheless, English is my main focus so I make sure that I do not slacken my English study.

Ethnic and cultural differences apparent In Japanese and English

Understanding a foreign language also means understanding the culture of the people who speak it, so that is extremely important. If you understand a language, you can understand the culture of its people; you become able to understand their history and the differences in their way of thinking. This is an extremely important point in learning a language.

There are even some people who say that my lectures are easier to understand in English than in Japanese [*laughs*]. There are people who say, "The structure of your English lectures is very logical and the conclusions are very clearly expressed, so the English-language lectures are easier to understand."

Japanese language uses roundabout expressions and nuances that cannot be clearly understood. In fact, people use expressions that are not crystal-clear in order to avoid any criticism. This is especially true of Japanese politicians, and newspaper companies usually "translate" their words into clearer language. When it comes to the Japanese language, unless the edge is taken off words, people would often clash, so Japanese is not a clear-cut language.

Even when my Japanese lectures are translated into English, they do not necessarily become more clear-cut. There are differences between giving lectures in English and giving lectures in Japanese to a Japanese audience. That is why, when Japanese is translated directly into English, just as it is, it does not always come out well.

At any rate, studying the thought patterns and cultures of people from other countries will provide you with a more developed perspective. It is probably important to do that in an earlier phase, before learning "an alien language" from aliens in space [*laughs*].

8
Study History to Become An Educated Person

When you become a working adult
You forget the history you learned at school

While languages are important to become an educated person, if possible it is a good idea to study history as well. We study history before entering university but most people have forgotten what they learned after a year at university. What is more, almost nobody studies history again later after entering the workforce.

Even if they occasionally read historical novels, most people are probably content to read one long book during the summer, for example on their summer vacation, because these books do take quite a long time to get through. However, you must continue to take an interest in history.

Although it may be hard to find the time to read books about history when you are busy with work, it is important to maintain this interest. You should read such books when you get the chance, little by little, otherwise you will lose your grasp on what you have learned. You will forget your knowledge of history, just as you forget math or a second language.

Speaking from my own experience, once you are over the age of 30, almost all the knowledge you acquired in your school days is lost. In your twenties, and particularly in your early twenties, when you see university test questions you think, "Hey! I could still do well if I studied again." However, that feeling fades rapidly when you reach the age of 30. You find yourself thinking that it is no longer possible to study this all over again, or rather that you would not be able to understand it even if you tried. That is how you feel once you get to 30.

On the other hand, you have acquired a lot of different knowledge. As a working adult you have a greater store of different knowledge and experience; lots of new information comes in and old information no longer springs to mind.

So please think of it like this: things that you learned previously will keep vanishing from your mind. It happens at a faster rate than you would expect. The more experiences you accumulate, the faster the old information will disappear, so you have to make an effort every so often to reclaim knowledge that you think you will need in the future.

If you do not know the history of your country
You will have a tough time overseas

When you go overseas, of course you will run into difficulties if you cannot speak a foreign language such as English. In addition to that, you will have a very tough time if you are unable to talk to people about your country.

If you have ever been stationed abroad or done a home-stay, or been on a trip, you will understand what I mean. Or if you have had an intellectual conversation with foreigners, you will understand how truly terrible it feels to be unable to say very much about your own country. You will then take an unexpected interest in your own country and have the urge to study it anew.

Of course, you have to be able to talk about modern affairs in your country and you also have to know about its history, which you have started to lose your grasp on. Even someone like me, who studied both Japanese history and world history to enter university, found it harder and harder to recall historical facts when I started to study many other things in my thirties. I could only vaguely remember Japanese history, for example, becoming unsure about the sequence of the eras.

Therefore sometimes you have to take an interest in these things. If you feel that your recollections are becoming vague, you should sometimes make an effort to read something like a simple guide for beginners—a paperback will do—in between other things, or occasionally read something like a historical novel.

A well-known Japanese author Ryotaro Shiba wrote many historical novels, novels that had very difficult subject matter. It is hard to believe that his books have been so widely read. His book, *Saka no Ue no Kumo* [Clouds Above the Hill] is a rather weighty tome of several volumes, and when I heard that it had sold nearly 20 million copies, I wondered if that was true, considering the population of Japan. Maybe some people bought it but did not actually read it.

If you like a certain author, you can commit yourself to that author and keep reading his or her books. By doing so, you will be able to get an overall picture of a subject; if it is a historical novel then you will get an overall picture of history. If you like their literary style and way of thinking, it is possible to keep on reading their works until you have read nearly everything they have written. So it is advisable to make that kind of effort.

Your recall of world history will also become fuzzy, so I advise you to make an effort to read different books about the countries you are interested in.

9

Leading an Intellectual Life That Enables You to Produce Intellectual Output

Innovation by uniting disparate elements

To become an educated person, you need to keep up your efforts to cultivate the specialized field related to your own work little by little, as well as other fields that are connected with it. You also need to dig a fountain of "language skills," acquire fresh perspectives and obtain new sources of information. Then, take an interest in a number of different subjects, such as foreign literature and history, and become able to tell people about your own country as well.

There are very few people nowadays who can do all this when they want to produce intellectual output, so if you continue "dabbling" in things that other people do not, that can sometimes lead to an entirely unique perspective.

As the management consultant Peter F. Drucker said, innovation is systematic scrapping, discarding old ways of doing things. To put it in scientific terms, innovation is a uniting of disparate elements. Innovation occurs when disparate elements unite, just as water is formed when hydrogen and oxygen unite. In the same way, if you have disparate elements and make an effort not to leave them merely to become miscellaneous information, your intellectual output will expand.

Many people who have studied the sciences in particular, are surprised when they see someone with a background in the humanities who possesses even the slightest knowledge of science. Even if that knowledge is something that people with a background in the sciences have studied as a matter of course, however trivial it may be, they tend to be really amazed and impressed by it. As far as I have observed, this is often the case.

Probably everyone knows about something like the Big Bang, but when someone with a background in the humanities comes out with terms such as "inflationary universe" or "parallel worlds," people who have studied the sciences start to get excited. Even if the person using it does not understand much about it, they are nevertheless very impressed and wonder how the person could know about something which only someone with a scientific background should be able to understand.

But that kind of knowledge can usually be acquired simply by reading books at the paperback level. If you are interested, you just need to read that kind of book occasionally, or read the articles sometimes found in the science column of newspapers. That kind of article can also be found in magazines like *Newsweek*, which is now translated into Japanese, so it is possible to read about fields other than your own.

Amass information and "crystallize" it

In this chapter I have mainly focused on how to study, but while browsing extensively through various fields you should always put one subject to the forefront and think about output, in other words, how to produce output in a tangible way. In fact, anyone can gather information if they make it a habit to do so, but it is very difficult to then "crystallize" it.

The story of the "Salzburg salt mine" is often cited on the subject of love. This comes from *De l'Amour* [On Love] by Stendhal, which I remember reading a long time ago. I remember reading the deft description, which says something like: "Love is like the 'flower' of Salzburg [a city in Austria]. When a bough is left in the salt mine, the salt turns to crystals, which attach themselves to the bough, like flowers. Love is not true unless it produces such crystals."

When it comes to intellectual output too, it is not enough simply to have the "salt"; the important thing is "how to crystallize it." To this end, some kind of motivation is needed. You need to have some kind of noble aspiration or wish, for example, "I want to use the knowledge I have to be of service to society, even in a small way," "I want to inspire people," "I want to serve as a guide to many people" or "I want to teach people troubled by the same problem how to resolve it." As long as you continue to have this aspiration, it is possible to lead an intellectual life that enables the production of intellectual output.

In order to produce intellectual output, Some kind of gentle exercise is also necessary

To finish, I would like to add one more point. At the start of this chapter I wrote that Kant adopted the habit of going for walks. When you are studying your body stiffens up and your shoulder muscles become tight. As well as that, your brain gets tired and your blood does not circulate properly. Bad circulation impairs your studying and your performance plummets.

Therefore, to improve your circulation you need to adopt some form of regular and repeated gentle exercise. It is best to do some kind of exercise you have done before, though ultimately you will probably end up just going for walks. If you get your body moving in this way, your intellectual performance can suddenly improve.

Generally speaking, when you find that you cannot read any more it is because your blood is not circulating properly. Lack of exercise is also the reason that students cramming for exams find that their study performance does not improve.

I know from my own experience that I can suddenly read books ten times faster when my circulation improves, and I feel that fatigue really does build up very easily. You should therefore make various efforts of this sort while producing intellectual output.

In this chapter, I have written rather generally about intellectual production. Although middle-aged people may find that a lot of what I have written here is common sense, I have included points that I felt young people will have learned for the first time. I hope that many of you will produce some output in the intellectual sphere in the near future.

Chapter Three

The Power to Break Through Walls

~ The Power of the Mind
That Defeats Negative Thinking ~

Lecture given on May 6, 2014
at Tokyo Shoshinkan
Tokyo, Japan

1
The Negative Thinking
That Strongly Pervades Japan

Many people have the tendency
To run into brick walls

The title of this chapter is "The Power to Break Through Walls," which seems to be an important issue for many people. In other words, many people apparently have a tendency to run into brick walls. While I rarely do so myself, many people find themselves facing a wall that blocks them. They are struggling with obstacles they have discovered within their own minds, and are unable to break through them.

Some of you may be praying to receive a magical bullet of "power to break through walls," so I will do my best to give you answers.

The pattern of moving from "negative thinking"
To "thinking that maintains the status quo"

First, I would like to state that Japanese people as a whole have a strong tendency toward negative thinking.

In other words, the Japanese have a very strong tendency to be pulled into negative thinking.

In many cases this negative thinking is then followed by a way of thinking that tries to maintain the status quo. First, they reject what is new or unknown, what has no precedent, and then adopt a way of thinking that maintains the status quo. Quite a lot of people probably fall into this pattern of thinking.

If you have this way of thinking, all new challenges seem like "walls." Whenever you try and start something new, everything seems like a wall, and you feel distress, wondering how you can get past that brick wall.

However, there are no textbooks that can provide answers to every one of the obstacles that each person encounters in life. You have no choice but to look at the opinions of the general public and the examples of other people, and find your own answers.

Despite that, because "thinking" is very difficult, people gradually want to deny making effort and eventually return to negative thoughts such as "I can't do it because it's too difficult. Things are fine as they are now, after all." The way I see it, this force is always operating in Japanese people as a whole.

The importance of "the capacity to estimate," Which can be learned from swimming across rivers

Taking up a new challenge is like trying to swim upstream against a river, or trying to swim in a straight line across a river. If you try to swim across a river in a straight line, you will always be swept along by the current and end up downstream. So if you want to arrive at the same point on the opposite side, you have to swim in a diagonal line upstream.

I say this based on my own experience. Unlike some children in modern times, I grew up surrounded by nature and often swam in the Yoshino River in Tokushima Prefecture, where I was born and raised. There were often "Danger" signs but from a young age, the existence of a risk increased my resolve, otherwise I would not have started this organization now [*laughs*].

When it comes to swimming across a river, as you develop the capacity to estimate and become able to calculate where on the other bank you will land according to how powerfully you swim, you become better and better at it. In the same way, in life it is important to gain "the capacity to estimate," the ability to perceive where you will end up if you continue your efforts, while battling against the various opposing forces that will arise. You need to be able to estimate where you will ultimately end up.

Replace excuses for not being able to do things With positive ideas

Today, Japanese people in general have a very strong tendency to list excuses why they cannot do something. If you have the same tendency, you need to make it a habit to hold it in check. In other words, it is important to acquire the habit of realizing that you often make excuses for being unable to do something, and replacing this with positive ideas.

The world is full of things that you cannot do. Generally speaking, laws and regulations bind people; all that is written in them is "You mustn't do this. You mustn't do that." For example, school rules and company regulations are all like that. They very rarely say, "You are allowed to do this."

Even if a company's internal rules state the limits of the jurisdiction of various positions, there is no mention of what every employee is allowed to do, and it is very rare to find company rules that outline what new employees are allowed to do. There are only rules that state someone's power of approval runs as far as X million dollars, or impose some other limit.

Out in society, there are also rules like "Minors must not smoke" and "Minors must not drink alcoholic beverages." But there are not many laws and regulations that cover what is acceptable to do. Therefore, you need to set out with the approach of "how to liberate yourself from negative regulations," otherwise things will not move forward.

The same can be said of myself too. An example is when I was to give a lecture on "The Power to Break Through Walls," which was then transcribed to become this chapter. The day before the lecture I was asked to give a talk that would help people from all walks of life break through their walls, for it was going to be relayed by satellite all over Japan. This made me think, "That's an extremely difficult request. Maybe the El Cantare-Belief Promotion Division [one of the divisions at Happy Science General Headquarters] is cutting corners."

So I said, "Oh! I think my eyes are a bit swollen. Maybe I won't be able to give the lecture tomorrow," and looked at my family. They all looked at me blankly without any sympathy [*audience laughs*]. When I was lying down and reading a book, I again said, "Oh! I think I've pulled a muscle in my left thigh. I might not be able to stand up tomorrow." Then my second daughter, who had just come home from the Happy Science Academy dormitory, brought me some ice. She told me that was how they cure it at the Academy cheerleaders dance club, and when she iced my leg it soon improved and I was able to stand on it.

None of my disciples believed any of my excuses for

not being able to give the lecture. I tried putting out a few feelers, asking "If I take the day off tomorrow, will you give the lecture instead of me?" but they all fell flat. So I too have many walls, in the sense that no one else can take my place.

Why a bank-bashing drama, which showed How to break through "impossible requirements," Became popular in Japan

The tendency to make excuses for not doing things generally becomes stronger as you get older. But this is also another side of wisdom. It is true that thinking "I mustn't do this or that" in anticipation of danger or failure at an early stage and avoiding it is another side of wisdom, or a type of solidified wisdom. However, when this sort of thinking becomes prevalent, it becomes an obstacle to moving things forward.

The same is true in schools and companies. While it is a problem if there are a lot of *don'ts*, if the requirement for a capable employee is how accurately a person has memorized those many don'ts, then the work of that institution as a whole will not progress. In a bank, for example, if the clerks are made to intensively study and memorize nothing but conditions for refusing to provide funds, they will develop a negative way of thinking. If they are punished for disobeying these, none of them will authorize any loans.

Recently in Japan, a bank-bashing drama aired repeatedly on TV. In a way, it is probably because there are many people who have had bad experiences at banks and can sympathize with the sentiments of the drama.

Even if people ask for loans, saying that their company will succeed and grow, banks usually do not believe them. Of course the bank will understand what they mean once they have actually demonstrated their success, but it is before that that they need the money. Although capital is required before they succeed, banks will not believe people when they outline their vision of success.

Banks want objective proof, so they start asking things like "Do you have any assets?" "Do you have any land?" or "Do you have life insurance?" Generally speaking, that makes most people lose motivation and start to think, "If that's the case, I'll stick with things the way they are. I'll just keep on renting." In many cases people tend to gradually retract in this way.

2
The Power to Think
That is Required of a Leader

Learning from the power
To break through resistance and survive,
Which works in the natural world

Various obstacles arise as you go through life, so it is important to consider how you can break through these with new ways of thinking.

Look at the natural world. For example, even if the ground has been surfaced with concrete or covered with asphalt, sometimes dandelions bloom and grass grows in the chinks and cracks. Sometimes when I see this, I am amazed at how they can find a way out through such tiny spaces.

Near where I live there is bamboo growing and I am amazed by the bamboo shoots too. In the growth season, they sprout from unexpected places and grow in sudden spurts. They know that they will be harvested and eaten if people find them, so they grow at a tremendous rate, understanding that they have to complete their growth before they are found.

There are only a few days when bamboo shoots are an edible size. If we miss that window they grow really quickly and become so tough that they do not taste good, and all we can do then is leave them to grow. Perhaps they too understand that they will lose their lives unless they have a growth spurt in that short time.

The power to break through resistance and survive is at work like this in the natural world as well. Of course, animals also have this tendency. All kinds of creatures put up a fight using their own particular "weapons."

However you look at it, the growth rate of the bamboo shoot is not reasonable. They emerge from the soil and grow to be fifteen to thirty feet high, but it certainly does not seem as if the soil contains sufficient materials for that growth. I cannot help but imagine that the soil below should sink in a bit when the bamboo gets that big, but it does not. Bamboo is hard so it cannot be all sap. I find it a real mystery and wonder just where its materials come from.

The power to think
Is the greatest weapon humans have

Animals too all have their own "weapons." They all have at least one special skill. For example, cats are actually rather timid, but physically they possess great agility, so even if they fall while walking along a wall, they will not die. It is very rare for them to die unless they fall in front of a car. If humans were to do the same thing they would break bones and be rushed to hospital, so in that sense, cats are superior to humans.

Rabbits have a habit of instinctively digging holes. We have quite a few rabbits in our home and, because there is nowhere to dig holes, they try their hardest to burrow into the carpet or the sofa. In their desperate attempt to refine their ability so that they do not lose it, they destroy the furniture. They are being fed to fulfill their original purpose of comforting their owner, but instead they just keep on energetically practicing their burrowing [*laughs*]. Perhaps it is because they are instinctively maintaining a way to survive in case they someday happen to be abandoned in the wild.

It is true to say that all creatures encounter various difficulties in their daily lives, but they have all been given some kind of "weapon" to overcome these.

Humans have many kinds of "weapons," as befits creatures that are called the "lords of creation." So, what is the greatest of those "weapons"? Although there are of course limits to physical strength, when it comes to the power to think there is considerable potential for growth and extensive scope for its application. In other words, the power to think creates scope and difference in humans. This aspect is strongly apparent in humans.

A leader must think ahead,
Not just focus on current tasks

Let me tell you what happened, as an example. When Happy Science was building its head temples in Tochigi Prefecture, between 1996 and 1998, we had already launched a project to build Tokyo *Shoshinkan**. However, the staff at General Headquarters actually lived in Utsunomiya at the time and so when I said we would build Tokyo Shoshinkan, they did not really absorb it.

I guess that when they are in Utsunomiya, they can only think about things connected to Utsunomiya. The plan was to build the first Shoshinkan in Utsunomiya, then build Miraikan, and then Nikko *Shoja**, so I guess they were completely occupied with how to run the first Shoshinkan successfully.

Meanwhile, I bought the land for Tokyo Shoshinkan and made plans to build it while we were at the stage where we were managing Utsunomiya Shoshinkan and had not yet built Miraikan or Nikko Shoja. But the staff just could not imagine it, however much I tried to persuade them. They could not think of anything other than running the head temples successfully before they could move on to the next step. At that time I really felt that they lacked the capacity to think about it.

---

* Shoshinkan and Shoja are temples of Happy Science. They are sacred places where prayers, religious training and worship take place.

However, once Tokyo Shoshinkan was built, they then became fixated on that. Their focus was then on running Tokyo Shoshinkan and they could not really grasp it when I told them that we were going to build shoshinkans throughout Japan. Maybe they could not see that it was possible. They ended up focusing on just one thing and did not have the power to think beyond that.

In terms of time too, our staff just did not seem to have the ability to think beyond the here and now. Even those who were said to be "highly capable" were like that.

Of course, there is the philosophy of "living each day as if it were your last," and it is important to do your very best each and every day. Common to all forms of business is the idea that you have to focus only on the task in hand. However, you cannot become a leader if you simply carry out the task you have currently been given.

Of course, going all out at the task at hand is one of the qualities of a leader, but to be a leader you must also think ahead and consider things that no one has considered yet. It is extremely important to always consider whether there are other possibilities, other methods, other businesses, or the seeds of other kinds of work, and not just be concerned with the task at hand.

3

Acquire Professional Skills

No one complains about
How much a professional earns

In addition, it is also important to expand into new areas and acquire the skills of a professional within those areas. Simply put, a professional is someone who does a job and gets paid for it. You are a professional when it is only natural that you should be paid. If you are not paid, you are an amateur. There is a clear difference between a professional and an amateur.

The same is true in sports like baseball. There are many people who like baseball. Some of them like to watch and some of them like to play. And there is, of course, a difference between an amateur and a pro. No one complains if a professional earns millions of dollars. That is because his earnings reflect how good of a job he is doing; the higher the earnings, the better his work.

People who do a good job are well rewarded, and no one complains about that. That is because professionals bring joy to many people. Professionals will naturally be treated with a certain amount of respect. However, if someone got paid a lot of money for playing sandlot baseball, people would surely feel he did not have the right to so much money.

Happy Science has gradually changed, Becoming able to work professionally

In that sense, when you start new businesses and move into new sectors, or when you take on challenges that you had been incapable of up until now, you are entering the world of the professional. It is a struggle for time and space until a person who has been part of a world of amateurs, becomes a professional.

Happy Science started out as a religion; initially it was mainly concerned with getting people to come and hear my lectures, seminars and training courses, so all our staff had to do was to inform people about events and prepare for them.

However, as we started building centers with accommodation for spiritual training like shoshinkans, their work gradually changed. Our staff was used to simply organizing events like lectures, so it was beyond their experience and they did not really know what to do. Because they had no experience of the hotel industry, they ended up building places that were like company offices and later had problems making them user-friendly. These kinds of problems occurred repeatedly many times. So, it is indeed very hard to become professional.

After running training centers for over ten years, though, the head ministers of the shojas started to gain confidence; they had mastered the techniques and had become competent at their jobs. When one person became able to do something, before long so did others. This sort of mysterious concatenation started to occur and gradually they turned into professionals. The work of amateurs has thus gradually changed into the work of professionals.

The Happy Science educational project Is becoming "professional" in a short time

When a religion first launches an educational project, in the beginning, of course it is amateur work and does not deserve financial compensation. So those in the organization must ask themselves, "How can we turn amateur work into professional? Where can we get that know-how? What efforts do we need to make? What kind of methods should we use, how should we manage people and what kind of results do we need to achieve, to be deserving of the title professional?" Unless these questions are explored, things will not go smoothly when a religion enters the educational project. They need to keep on acquiring new skills while asking themselves at what point they become professionals.

Today Happy Science runs the Happy Science Academy junior high and high schools in the Nasu Main School and in the Kansai School, as well as the Buddha's Truth cram school named "Success No.1." We are thus gradually amassing know-how in the education business. Furthermore, we are now making preparations for the establishment of the Happy Science University. [At the end of October 2014, the Ministry of Education, Culture, Sports, Science and Technology refused approval for the establishment of Happy Science University. Although we will call for the refusal to be withdrawn, we are planning to open a religious institution for higher education, Happy Science University (HSU) in April 2015.]

In general, people may think that Happy Science is still inexperienced in the world of education, but there are also people who are amazed at the speed with which Happy Science has demonstrated professionalization in a short space of time.

We must, of course, become professional. We will encounter stiff resistance as we break new ground and develop our professionalism from the ground up, but we have to overcome that.

We have to find answers to the issues, "What is the meaning in setting out to establish a new university in an age when the university business is faltering because there are too many of them? How much potential is there?" How to answer these questions is one of the walls before us. Whether we can break through it or not depends on how the students who enter and pass through HSU then go on to live.

4

I Want to Create Japanese Who Break the Mold of The Typical Japanese

Building a school that can open up Students' potential

While we are aiming to establish the HSU, there are already plenty of other famous universities. At the Happy Science Academy and Success No.1 we have been teaching the know-how to enter those universities. But when HSU opens and the Happy Science Academy becomes an "escalator school," what should we do?

Schools that prepare their students for university entrance exams and schools whose students can automatically move up to a university may well have different cultures. Most of the existing escalator schools end up as places where students mainly take life easy and become lazy in their studies, since they do not need to study hard for university entrance exams.

However, it is important to set up an educational environment where the longer they are in that environment, the more the students' potential as human beings opens up, and that these students become able to introduce approaches and ways of thinking for a new world. Our challenge is whether we can create such a learning environment.

In any case, in Happy Science various activities are now moving forward at a speed that has exceeded our expectations and we are gaining deeper confidence.

Our role as an opinion leader
To change common way of thinking in Japan

What is more, we have to transform commonly accepted understandings in Japan. So what are the factors that create commonly accepted understandings in Japan? One factor is education, another is politics, and another is the reporting of the mass media. Happy Science therefore transmits different kinds of information from a media-like vantage point, and is making efforts to take on the role of opinion leader, or trendsetter, and trying to open up a path.

We are now preparing to open a religious institution for higher education, HSU, and as it produces graduates every year, the society will have no choice but to accept them. And once those graduates start working at different companies, our religion will take root more widely in society and become better recognized. Moreover, by looking at the work of those graduates, in jobs that are being assessed by general society, people who have felt a kind of resistance or had some fear of religion can learn about the nature of that religion through those "windows."

An education that can produce people with the wish To "enrich" the whole world

While Happy Science is currently reforming education, the mass media and politics, and also planting the next "seeds" overseas, what I find most regrettable is that there are very few things "originating from Japan" that have a global influence.

The Japanese have always being told that they are good at importing things from other countries, which they then build upon and improve. However, there are no cases of foreign countries developing and prospering on the basis of new inventions exported from Japan. There may be a few if you look hard enough, but I think there are almost no such cases.

For example, Toyota cars may outsell American ones but the company in Japan just improved cars that were originally from the U.S. and won their market share by beating the competition in terms of cost and performance. However, I do not feel that is enough.

It would be great if Japan could present a way of overcoming the world's problems or difficulties by using methods that were first thought up and launched in Japan. That would be momentous work.

So I want to create a totally new breed of humanity at the HSU. I am planning to create "Japanese who are un-Japanese." I am trying to invent an educational institution that can produce people who break the mold of the typical Japanese, people who have been born to become global-minded from the very start and people with the wish to "enrich" the whole world.

The resolution of builders to construct a temple That will change the world

The other day I went to take a look at the site where we are planning to build the HSU in Chiba Prefecture. The big construction company that built our Happy Science Academies in Nasu and Kansai was in charge of building the university as well, and the same person who was responsible for both academies was also there to take charge of the university. So he lived in the Nasu area, then on the shores of Lake Biwa in Kansai area, and now he has moved to Kujukuri Beach in Chiba Prefecture and continues to build for us.

As he feels responsible, he planted a sign at the construction site that said in large letters, "We hereby vow to be the very best temple carpenters." In other words, the construction people are working in the spirit of constructing, not a school, but a temple.

When I saw that I felt, "That's a commendable attitude!" I was really impressed by their resolution, "We're not building a school. We're building a temple." We are planning to build a pyramid-shaped prayer hall so, of course, it is true to say that it is like a temple, but I was delighted to see that they are approaching their work with the attitude that this is no ordinary school. I believe that they are not just constructing buildings but probably praying that the people who study there will go on to do great things, and become leaders of Japan and change the world.

Meanwhile, as I gazed across the vast expanse of land where the buildings are being constructed, I was deeply moved by how far we have come in 10, 20, 30 years. I once said that it would probably be impossible for us to get as far as building a school in my lifetime. However, even though I said it was probably impossible, once I started to think about it, that reality could be drawn closer.

Even if you consider something to be impossible to achieve, if you continue making efforts thinking, "No, it may be possible after all," you will find that it gradually takes shape. As you think about what it is that you can do, and hammer away steadily at it, almost before you realize, it will become a source of strength for you.

5

Aspirations Open Up a Path

The effects of education experienced Through my English-language teaching materials

Furthermore, when I thought about what I could do, I decided to restart my English studies in tandem with overseas missionary work. While doing this, I started out by tackling things like creating English textbooks, which then led to improvements in the English skills of various people within our organization, such as those involved in overseas missionary work or education projects.

For example, when we started doing full-scale overseas missionary work a few years ago, I gave lectures in English at Happy Science Headquarters partly for my own practice. At that time, when we gathered the headquarters staff, those who had a high level of English competency, like those who had a TOEIC score of more than 800 or staff from our International Headquarter, usually sat in the front two rows. There were only 18 of them, while the rest had not achieved that level.

Now, however, [as of May 2014] there are 70 or 80 people with a TOEIC score of more than 900, and nearly 200 who have a score of over 800. So, through the effects of education their ability has increased ten-fold, or even more.

Using numerous English textbooks that I created, there was a pupil at the Happy Science Academy who passed the EIKEN* Grade Pre-1 in their first year at junior high. They may be a little too intelligent. I wonder what to teach them next; maybe they should now move on to study at university.

Generally speaking, passing the EIKEN Grade Pre-1 makes it possible for working adults to get an overseas post; that is the kind of level we are talking about. To be able to work overseas, people usually need to study practical English after graduating from university. So I was stunned to hear that a first-year pupil at junior high school had achieved that level.

And there was something else that astonished me. My second daughter, who is my fifth child, entered the Happy Science Academy. My older children went to a typical Japanese school that focuses on getting its pupils into prestigious university, but in fact it was my fifth child who passed the EIKEN Grade 2 exam at her first attempt when she was in her second year at junior high school.

---

* An English language test created to improve the English skills of Japanese people. It is supported by the Japanese Ministry of Education, Culture, Sports, Science and Technology.

Apparently her self-image was that she was the least intelligent of her siblings, but other siblings who were at the level of the so-called "big three" private junior and senior high schools in Japan [Kaisei, Azabu and Musashi] did not pass EIKEN Grade 2 at that stage. So I was amazed and wondered how she managed to pass it so quickly.

When I saw these sorts of results, I was able to affirm that the teaching materials I had created were not so bad after all.

English Vocabulary and Phrase Book *goes beyond The level of the "big three" private junior And senior high schools*

I also created the *English Vocabulary and Phrase Book* series for people preparing for university entrance examinations. The other day, when my third son [a freshman at the University of Tokyo] gave a talk at Success No.1 [refer to Yuta Okawa, *Risouteki Na Juken Seikatsu No Okurikata* (The Ideal Lifestyle When Preparing for University Entrance Examinations), (Tokyo: Happy Science, 2014)], he introduced the green-covered *Success No.1 English Vocabulary and Phrase Book, Essential Edition for Passing the University Entrance Exam.* He said that when he showed it to his friends at school they were all startled by how many of the words in it they did not know.

I make it a habit to get hold of English vocabulary and phrase books that are used by other cram schools and take a look through them. Even the books from what I think to be the highest-level cram school called *Tetsuryokukai*, attended by pupils of the "big three" high schools and taught by students of the University of Tokyo, are simpler than I expected. They create tests based on such simple-level texts, so it is clear that Success No.1 is way ahead of them. Our students are studying content that would make the people at Tetsuryokukai say, "Wow! They're covering things like this. This is really difficult."

When it comes to English idioms, none of the university entrance exam reference books to be found in Japan at the moment are at the level of my series, *English Vocabulary and Phrase Book*. Therefore I think that it is only natural that the pass rate of people who have studied it should go up.

Opening up a path with the greatest talent: The ability to aspire

It is important to construct a plan, ask yourself what you can do to achieve it, and then put it into practice little by little. As you continue doing that you will accumulate a certain amount, which then becomes systemized and arranged in stages. Then various people will be able to move from step 1 to step 2, and from step 2 to step 3.

Each individual task may be tedious work. However, if you start by attacking it from the angle of your strong point and create a path, you will find a specific way of doing things. Once you achieve this, people in other fields will start to collaborate with you, inspired by your work. This collaboration will open up various channels and your work will proceed to completion.

It is not so easy to be good at everything. But, just as in the examples of animals I mentioned earlier, if you find your own strong points and create innovation using them, this will become a force that propels you into new businesses and new worlds. This is essential.

Human beings have the capacity to succeed if they try. There is a time-honored saying, "It's never too late to learn." When I was young they were just words to me, but now I really do see that actually there is nothing that cannot be done if you try.

You can expand your abilities as far as you want, be you 50, 60 or 70. You can open up new fields. You have to restrain yourself so that you do not become a mere daydreamer, but if you steadily build on your strong points and make efforts, you will move beyond the level you were at when you were young, then beyond a certain high level, and then you will definitely climb far beyond. Then if you produce new ideas based on those results, the number of people who are following you, or who collaborate with you, will gradually increase, so you will become capable of a big project.

Above all, will power and aspiration are important. The ability to aspire is the greatest gift. The path only opens up through strong aspiration, "I want to do this! I want to be like this! I want to try this! I want to get this far!"

The very fact that aspiration emerges from within is in itself a gift. What is emerging from within you now? What is emerging is your gift. Having that gift means that such a possibility exists.

6
The Power of Management
To Break Through Walls

The functions of management can be summed up
As marketing and innovation

The management consultant, Peter F. Drucker, wrote a great many books about management, and he himself provides a simple summary of them. First of all, when it comes to the basic nature of management, he says that one of its functions is marketing.

Marketing means getting the customer to use things that are on the market, such as products and services. As work, marketing means increasing the number of people who use a service or buy a product.

He says that another function of management is innovation. This is the power to constantly change things in accordance with different management circumstances.

In short, Drucker says, "Management consists of two functions: marketing and innovation. There is nothing else worth speaking of." So basically, if you want to break down walls, you should use both marketing and innovation.

The wall that you are facing may be in a family business or a job in a company. Or in terms of religious work, it could be in missionary work activities, in giving people books of Truth, or in Happiness Planting [making donations]. However, I can say conclusively that marketing is one of the things that you should do. By this I mean making many people aware of the value of a product or service, and getting them to accept it.

The other thing you need to put into practice is innovation. Different things come up, depending on the stage you are at in your work. Various things will come up, for example, the concepts and ideas you have to implement next, how to manage people, how to make use of new employees, or a stage where you have to find people to collaborate with. Each time you need the power of innovation to allow your thinking to evolve.

As long as you are armed with these two functions, you will surely make progress in your work, be it work for a company or work outside a company, such as volunteer or NPO work.

It is important to teach people who up until now have not wanted a product or service, or people who did not think that they needed religious faith, that it is in fact necessary and get them to accept it. That is marketing.

And then, according to the stage they are at, teach them about new products and services, and new ways of thinking, while at the same time evolving your own methods. That is innovation.

Fighting with these two weapons to break through walls is the pathway for a large organization to move forward.

It is a leader's mission to think constantly About working effectively

I always think as much as possible about how one task can be employed in two or three ways. I think about how work that is done for one particular purpose can also be applied to other things.

I think about how various tasks can be used in many different ways, for example, how something that I did for the Happy Science Academy could then be used for overseas missionary work, or how something I did for overseas missionary work could be used for your companies. In this way, I always think about how results can be multiplied many times over. I believe that it is the mission of a leader to think like this constantly, about how to build work to be effective.

In this chapter, I have made introductory and general remarks on the theme of "the power to break through walls." I ask you all to break down the walls that you are up against now. While the Bank of Japan is now conducting so-called "other-dimensional" monetary easing, saying that it is quantitative and qualitative easing in a different dimension, it is Happy Science that can exert the real "other-dimensional power." Let us make the other-dimensional power work at Happy Science.

Chapter Four

An Other-Dimensional Way of Thinking

~ How to Have Ideas
That Transcend This World ~

Lecture given on February 11, 2014
at Tokyo Shoshinkan
Tokyo, Japan

1
What is an Other-Dimensional Idea?

People have different needs for
An other-dimensional way of thinking

This chapter has the extremely other-dimensional title of "An Other-Dimensional Way of Thinking." My readers may have various expectations about its content and it is very difficult to provide information that will fulfill everybody's needs.

A business owner may be looking for ideas for his work as company president, while a businessman may be trying to find methods to break through the problems currently confronting him. Students may have hit a plateau in their studies or be worrying about whether a path will open up for them in the future. A housewife may be confronted with various household problems and wonder whether some kind of other-dimensional power might work to resolve them. In this way, there are a variety of needs.

While it is not possible to answer each problem individually and there may not be a solution that is exactly right for you, I am sure that just by being exposed to the contents of this chapter, something is going to change for you from this point on. In any case, I intend to provide assistance for getting other-dimensional ideas that correspond to your individual situation.

When you think about what an other-dimensional way of thinking is, perhaps you have an image of obtaining some form of guidance or inspiration from a world that transcends this worldly level, that opens up the path to success.

Actually, the way I work is basically the practice of this "other-dimensional way of thinking." However, it is not possible to make the details of this clear. Since it is other-dimensional it is not easy to explain, so I will try to translate this other-dimensional way of thinking into a three-dimensional context and reveal it to you.

Although many people may simply think that they can resolve problems once they have received various kinds of inspiration from Heaven, in actuality things are not that simple. While it is true that there are many guiding spirits in the heavenly world, certain conditions are necessary for you to receive the appropriate advice and guidance from those guiding spirits. If you want to solve your immediate problems with the help of their advice and guidance, and open the door to the future, you need to fulfill the appropriate conditions. In other words, it rarely happens that all the answers for you rain down upon you from Heaven, just like that.

So, in this chapter I want to describe ways to bridge other-dimensional ideas and three-dimensional ideas.

The law of cause and effect is also at work When you attract other-dimensional power

So what is an "other-dimensional idea"?

Thinking about it, whenever I intend to do something, I am not trying to receive inspiration and advice from the higher realms of the Spirit World in the form of an other-dimensional idea. Rather, in most cases I have forgotten about it. When I am acting under my own efforts, forgetting such things, it often turns out that in fact I am being helped.

This truly is a mysterious thing. Even though power does not come down from other dimensions in situations where something is impossible without that power, in situations that I can handle by myself, even without the assistance of that power from other dimensions, I am flooded with it. I can only say that it truly is mysterious.

For example, when I am persevering to do something without any such assistance, I start to receive all sorts of unasked-for guidance. However, in situations where I really am at a total loss and cannot do anything unless I receive some guidance, surprisingly it just does not come.

It really is a mysterious thing. It seems to me that concealed in this fact is a key to turn situations around. It is similar to the time-honored saying: "Heaven helps those who help themselves." It really is very much like that.

In other words, often I receive the most power from other dimensions when I am not aware of it, while strangely enough it does not seem to come at times when I think things like, "I really wish I could receive some power. Why doesn't it come? I could do this if it did." This may seem a bit cruel, but there is no negative intent: that is just the reality.

Thus the law of cause and effect, known as "the law of arising from causation," is also at work when it comes to attracting power from other dimensions.

Power comes from other dimensions
When preparations in this world are complete

It is the way people live and think in this world that creates the conditions for that law to work. As we can see from reading scriptures like the Old Testament, people do not choose to receive prophecies; in most cases these just suddenly come to them. When it appears that the preparations are complete or the time is ripe, such spiritual phenomena are most likely to occur and it is seldom possible for people on earth to choose them.

So power comes from other dimensions when you feel preparations are complete or the time is ripe. You have to consistently make preparations for this time. You need to be prepared at any moment so that you are ready to hear a voice from the heavenly world. That is to say, you have to be in a state where you are always ready and waiting in case inspiration should descend upon you and say, "Get to your feet now! Take action now! Do such and such now!" It is mostly in times of readiness that inspiration comes to you.

2
How to Get Other-Dimensional Ideas

1) Be someone who makes a habit of thinking

I would now like to state a few points about these prerequisites.

To put it in worldly terms, an other-dimensional idea is one that suddenly comes to you, the flash of inspiration that comes to you when, for example, you are thinking about planning or putting forward some proposal. The next issue is what you do with this flash of inspiration, but first, there is a condition that needs to be fulfilled in order to be able to receive such inspiration. The first prerequisite is to be someone who thinks deeply about things. You must be constantly contemplating things.

When it comes to this "thinking," it requires a certain amount of character building and personal effort to reach the level where you can recognize objectively that you are now actually thinking. You need to put in intellectual effort and spend time training your mind.

2) Acquire the seeds and materials for thinking

In order to reach a state where you are always thinking about something without your realizing it, you need to train yourself to think, and to do this you need the seeds and materials for thinking. In other words, "thought training" and "materials for thought" are needed.

3) Continue to make worldly efforts

In regard to this, you need to be aware that people who neglect to make an effort in a three-dimensional, worldly sense will not be able to receive good quality inspiration. That is to say, an other-dimensional way of thinking does not just suddenly come to you like an unexpected windfall.

For example, you will not constantly be visited by inspiration such as, "If you buy a lottery ticket now you will win five million dollars." Inspiration will come in a more sensible way. In most cases, when you are making the proper efforts, it will come within the scope of those efforts. So you are being watched attentively.

For example, there are many Olympic athletes who train with all their might. Subjectively, they may think that they have trained hard day in and day out, and pushed themselves to their very limit. But the question is: how are their efforts viewed from the heavenly world?

When a spirit in the heavenly world thinks, "This person has pushed himself to his very limits. It would be fine to send him a miracle now," it sometimes happens that a gymnast, for example, will be able to do a magnificent somersault, an "other-dimensional somersault." The spirit may help him spin round one additional time, and a miracle occurs.

Of course, for this kind of miracle to happen, as a prerequisite the person has to have endured very rigorous training on a daily basis, and also have developed the capacity to receive such a miracle. So you have to make the effort and develop your capacity to a certain level on your own.

4) There is a difference between happiness And good luck

When it comes to being happy, there are people who say that there is a difference between happiness and good luck. For example, a certain TV program talked about a theory being taught at Harvard University that said, "Statistically speaking, in a particular area, winning the lottery had no correlation with happiness."

Certainly, winning the lottery itself may be a good thing because you get money from it, but whether or not that brings happiness depends on the person concerned, so we cannot really say whether it is a good thing or not. Sometimes winning the lottery makes people lazy, or leads to them being robbed, or to their leading a flashy life and their eventual downfall.

So, in some ways happiness is not the same as good luck. When good luck comes your way after you have worked to create the capacity to receive it, it adds to and manifests as your actual competence.

3
The Ryuho Okawa Style of Other-Dimensional Thinking

The truth about Ryuho Okawa's writings, That is thought to require a staff of at least 500

With regard to an other-dimensional way of thinking, if outsiders look at my work, for example, they would probably imagine that I am using methods of working that are not of this world. Apparently a leading figure in the Japan Self-Defense Force once said that, judging by the number of books and policies I produce, I must have a staff of around 500 [see Ryuho Okawa, *Ryuho Okawa: Political Revolutionary* (New York: IRH Press, 2014)].

I can certainly see why he thought that it would be impossible to produce books of that quality and quantity without a staff of 500 frantically doing research and helping to write them. However, although it is true to say that a group of around 500 guiding spirits is hard at work in the heavenly world, I do not have 500 staffers working away in this world. I am simply continuing to do what needs to be done.

Simple efforts to receive other-dimensional power

1) Make efforts to expand the scope of Your interests

So what is it that I simply continue to do? One thing is that I am constantly making an effort to expand the scope of my interests. As well as that, I am always interested in new things.

It is indeed true that I am constantly observing so that I will not miss the beginnings of developments that will become trends in the future. But not only that, I am also learning the necessary lessons from people in history who have faced a similar situation or have overcome a similar obstacle to myself, and studying how they overcame the hardship.

2) Make efforts to expand your field of expertise

Furthermore, I am also expanding my area of expertise as a "wellspring of ideas."

Looking at Japan as a whole, there are said to be probably around 10,000 people who can have some sort of spiritual experience, such as receive some form of spiritual message from the Spirit World, hear voices, speak in tongues or receive spiritual visions. If we include "minor gods," such as shamans and so on, it may be true that there are about 10,000 people.

However, there are not many of them who go as far as to make it their profession. Even though they may be able to hear and speak with spirits, unless they have certain worldly abilities, it is impossible for them to produce such a wide range of books, or to have such a grand and profound perspective as Happy Science. Even though a shaman in the Aomori region [the northern part of Japan] may be genuine, it would be rather difficult for the spirits of Keynes or Hayek to descend through him or her.

Make efforts to become a semi-professional In various fields

Moreover, the spirits of scientific experts also send me spiritual messages. So, even if I do not have all that much specialized knowledge about science, I have to open my mind to scientific fields as well and plough my own field as much as I can, otherwise I will not be able to receive such messages.

Thus, someone like myself, who leans slightly more to the humanities side, may not be the best match when it comes to receiving inspiration from scientists in the Spirit World such as Einstein, Edison or Hideki Yukawa.

They probably think, "Isn't there someone somewhere more suitable, like a real Doctor of Science, who can receive spiritual messages?" But such scientists are most unlikely to be open to the spiritual and so are not able to receive spiritual messages.

However, even someone like me with a background in the humanities can also become capable of somehow understanding what they are saying, even if he is not entirely the same level as the experts. If you keep on studying year after year, with the determination to come closer to them and become someone who can hear their voices, once you reach the level where you would be able to understand a university lecture, you will be capable of receiving spiritual messages that fall within that range.

Their spiritual messages are filtered through my understanding so the opinions of scientific geniuses can be read and understood within the framework of a general understanding in society. The majority of people are not scientific experts, so they can benefit from these non-specialist descriptions.

So, even if you cannot get as far as a professional level in various fields, you have to make efforts to reach a level close to semi-professional, because unless your capacity is sufficient, you cannot receive messages.

How to develop the capacity to receive
Sufficient spiritual guidance from great composers

A while ago in Japan, there was a controversy surrounding someone who feigned deafness and was called "a modern-day Beethoven." As for myself, I can summon the spirits of Beethoven, Chopin and Mozart. However, even if they were to enter my body and play the piano, my fingers would not move properly.

If it were someone who had done a certain amount of practice and had reached the level of a concert pianist, they would be able to play as if divinely possessed and would even be able to compose at will. However, I have not done that much training and so cannot do that.

When composers today hear this, they probably feel regret and think, "If only they came down to me I could do it" but things do not happen that easily in this world. The world would no longer be in its rightful state if Mozart or Beethoven kept popping up all over the place, so there have to be limits to such things.

Sometimes narrow views of religion
Reject spiritual guidance

The spirits of religious figures will sometimes also appear, but to receive their messages you must have the capacity to understand their thinking and their feelings. I myself receive spiritual messages from various religious leaders.

Generally speaking, there are many religions that are focused upon one sutra or one way of thinking, and many people who believe in a religion like that, which has only one orientation, often reject other religions. For example, if a minister or priest who has done his spiritual training in Christianity develops a spiritual disposition, even if spiritual beings from religions other than Christianity send him some different kinds of teaching, he will say, "That cannot be possible" and reject them.

Apparently that is also true of Edgar Cayce, who was called the "sleeping prophet." When Edgar Cayce had shorthand notes taken of what he said under hypnosis, there were a lot of descriptions of reincarnation. Christianity considers the idea of reincarnation to be heresy and within it no such teaching exists, but all he talked about under hypnosis was reincarnation. So, while Edgar Cayce talked about reincarnation when he was in a hypnotic trance, when he was awake, at places like Sunday schools he would teach, "There is no such thing as reincarnation."

There can be slight differences in how messages are sent down depending on whether the living person can accept them or not. Sometimes such messages can be sent when the surface consciousness is asleep, as with Cayce. Perhaps the true nature of his soul was such that he had the capacity to receive such messages, even though he learned in Christianity that reincarnation does not exist and he did not believe in the idea at the level of his surface consciousness. While he was asleep, he even talked of the existence of the Age of Atlantis and the Age of Mu.

As for a business owner, guiding spirits That match his or her capacity will come

It is therefore essential to make efforts to develop your capacity. The same can be said about work. The extent to which you can increase your capacity will determine the extent to which your future prospects and potential will expand.

If you are the owner of a company, you have to think about what your vision for the future of your company is, and about the abilities required at each stage, according to your vision of the future. And when you make an effort to plough your own field in the direction which requires certain skills, a guiding spirit appropriate to the scale of your company will come to guide you in that direction. Furthermore, other guiding spirits will take over as the size of your company changes, and the right guiding spirit suitable for the scale of your enterprise will come.

The anguish of a manga artist with a creative block

Writers and other creators have to create works in various ways, but when creative energy ceases to well up in their minds, they run out of "seeds," which must surely cause them great anguish.

For this lecture, I read several books about the creation of ideas, one of which was about the manga artist Mr. Fujiko F. Fujio's way of coming up with ideas. I read it because I was interested in what he would say. Although there was almost nothing that was helpful for me personally, there was an interesting passage, saying the longest period that he had shut himself away to draw manga non-stop was 73 hours.

He wrote, "I left my food and water beside me and just kept on drawing. The longest I have drawn non-stop is 73 hours, which I have done only twice. Towards the end of that time the paper looked as though it was undulating." I thought, "Ah, so that's what it's like."

Moreover, when he could not draw anything even after shutting himself away, he would flee to Takaoka, his hometown in Toyama Prefecture. Apparently his editor could not pursue him that far but would send telegrams demanding his manuscripts.

Something similar was described in a book by the manga artist, Mr. Osamu Tezuka. Editors from various magazines would crowd into his living room urging him to write and draw, but if there were four or more of them at once, he could not respond to all their requests. Because he was unable to draw, he would pretend he needed to go to the toilet, escape through the toilet window, then go and hide in a movie theater and watch a movie. In other words, he would "disappear."

From these examples you can see that it is very hard when you have nothing left to draw or say, when you experience a creative block.

The second and later works of authors Who write books based on personal experiences Are less interesting

The same can be said of novelists as well. Every year sees new winners of the Naoki Prize and the Akutagawa Prize in the field of literature in Japan,* and when those writers win the award they are soon asked to deliver a second book, so most of them have already started work on a second book before they receive the prize.

---

* The Naoki Prize and the Akutagawa Prize are both prestigious Japanese literary awards established in 1935, named after prominent novelists Ryunosuke Akutagawa and Sanjugo Naoki respectively. The Naoki Prize goes to a writer of popular literature, while the Akutagawa Prize is awarded to a new author of serious literature.

However, there are quite a lot of novelists who, even though they have won the award, are unable to write anything more after their third book.

Their first novel may be based upon their personal experience and they may have distinctly interesting things to write. They may produce something that amazes the general public and makes people think, "This is great. I've never had that kind of experience." But when it comes to their second and third novels, the content becomes less and less compelling or interesting, and fewer people read them. This is particularly common with authors who write about personal experiences. It is often the case that their first book is the most interesting, and it is all downhill after that.

Mr. Ryu Murakami, who is currently the host of the TV program called "Cambria Palace," wrote various things about totally original experiences, experiences that people could not believe were possible, when he made his debut as an author in late 1970s. Even if you have never read these, you do not need to worry about it since there is no need to read such old books now. Works like his may have been interesting at the outset, since they were about something unusual that no one in the culture at that time has experienced.

For example, a book about an author's experience of narcotics might have been interesting in a time before drugs became common in Japan, just as writing about people who flouted convention when there were strict rules about relations between the sexes can sometimes be rather interesting. In the same way, writing a kind of confession about something "not permitted" in a certain line of work would be intriguing as well. However, the interest gradually wanes in their second and third books. That is the disadvantage of experience-based books.

Uninspired books based on documents Are uninteresting

In contrast to these, there are authors who should be described as "documentarians." When it comes to authors who gather up documents and data on which to base their writing, relatively few of them run out of themes. However, some of them are clearly "uninspired."

They can no doubt gather as much material as they want. They can get things from bookshops and other places, and now there is also plenty of data to obtain from sources like the Internet. However, if it is clearly obvious that they are simply writing something based on those materials alone and the writing lacks inspiration, there is somehow a sense that it is lacking in added value. That is why, when people read it, it somehow fails to capture their interest.

Reportage-style writings of collected facts can make for an interesting read if other people do not know about them, or if they happen to be on an unusual theme. But as the author continues to write, his writing will lose its interest value since readers will be able to get a general idea of the source of the information.

As well as just gathering and sorting information, You also need to "crystallize" it

It may be rather rude to actually name names but take, for example, someone like Mr. Takashi Tachibana,* who has become an expert and is now in his twilight years (at the time of the lecture). He is one of the giants of journalism and has written many "meaty" books, but when I read them I get the impression that in some ways he seems to think that processing information is the essence of wisdom. He seems to think that "wisdom" means to gather, sort and process information.

He is a good investigator and can quote from various sources, but his works somehow lack content that engages the reader. To put it in my words, there is a lack of "crystallization." Simply put, although the books themselves are of value as resources, they are slightly uninteresting.

---

* Takashi Tachibana (1940-2021) is a Japanese journalist, writer and critic. He is also known as an avid reader who possesses tens of thousands of books.

One of Mr. Tachibana's best-selling books is said to be one that records in documentary style the interview process by which he selected his secretary, something along the lines of "as many as 500 people applied when Takashi Tachibana advertised for a secretary" [*Boku wa Konna Hon wo Yonde Kita* (I have read these books)]. But other substantial works apparently have not sold particularly well.

That secretary worked for him for a while, but eventually ended up being fired because Mr. Tachibana's income fluctuated according to whether or not he was writing a book and apparently he became unable to pay his secretary her salary of 200,000 yen a month.

That was probably what made her angry. Takashi Tachibana's former secretary published a book in Okinawa criticizing him. She wrote criticisms such as, "It's unforgivable for a celebrated expert to fire someone because he can't pay them 200,000 yen, especially as his book about me was the one that had the best sales."

Allow the information you have gathered To ferment and mature

These days, Mr. Masaru Sato, who left the Ministry of Foreign Affairs and was imprisoned for a while, works in a fairly similar way to Mr. Tachibana. Certainly I can see that he probably reads a variety of books, but his information has not fermented. In my opinion, he often does not get as far as fermenting and distilling it as a creative work, but stops at the level where it is still just material.

Unfortunately, you cannot ultimately achieve intellectual success simply by gathering together materials. If you mix together rice and *koji* [a kind of mold], add water and stir, it will gradually produce alcohol and it will start to smell of Japanese sake. That kind of fermentation is lacking, and I cannot help but feel sometimes as if I am simply eating the raw materials.

Also, in one of Mr. Sato's recent books he writes about how a certain teacher told him to come to his cram school, trying to "recruit" him when he was in his second or third year at junior high school. His book includes conversations between a cram school instructor who had previously taught at a university in the former USSR and the then-junior high school student Mr. Sato, but I cannot help but feel that some of them are fabrications.

There is no way that a junior high school student could hold a conversation at that high of a level. I could soon see that it was written adding things that Mr. Sato had studied after joining the Ministry of Foreign Affairs. I do not think that even I could have spoken at that level in my third year at junior high. It is clear that he has transposed his current knowledge onto the past.

Therefore, even if a writer can gather all the necessary documents and materials, he will not ultimately succeed if they are not fermented sufficiently. People who become great writers study hard, and in most cases they give what they have learned time to ferment and, by combining it with various other things, let it go through a proper maturation process so that it comes out as something else. In that sense, many of them are probably the type of people who can do short-distance sprints and also run long distances.

Most of my ideas also come from such sources. Of course I study current events as well so that I can make journalistic judgments, but I am also constantly thinking about the future and the past based on those judgments. An example of how I study the past is that I think about how things would appear if I were living in a certain era.

You can acquire an international perspective by Studying languages

You also need to have an international perspective. For example, even when I criticize today's China, since it has a long history, I study things like Chinese works of art and literature to find out what kind of country China is. Therefore, when I make comments I do so with good knowledge of the temperament and way of thinking of the Chinese people, and how they will react to my comments.

Strangely enough, however, they do not know much about Japan. They know nothing about Japanese history. The same could be said about South Korea.

If you do research into other countries in this way, you can sometimes gain interesting perspectives when you talk about your own country as well. In that sense, studying subjects like foreign languages is intellectually stimulating. At the same time it will cause very valuable ideas to well up, because you will be able to acquire a perspective that enables you to see your own country as people from other countries see it.

There are tremendous benefits to acquiring competence beyond a certain level, but if you cannot, the benefits are minimal; they will be at the level of being able to pass exams. But, if you continue studying far beyond that level, you will become able to read about global trends in the early stage and understand what kind of nation your own country should become.

In that sense, looking at the results of the February 2014 Tokyo gubernatorial election, it is not a bad thing for a leader of Japanese local government to be knowledgeable about other countries. [The winner of this election was Mr. Yoichi Masuzoe, a scholar of international politics, who served as the Minister of Health, Labour and Welfare in 2007 and 2008.*]

---

* When Mr. Yoichi Masuzoe was young, he lived and studied in France and later became an assistant professor at the University of Tokyo, specializing in politics, diplomacy and security in European nations.

Someone who has lived in foreign cities and studied life in other countries will see Tokyo in a different light, and is probably a wellspring of ideas about what needs to be done where. That is not a bad thing, and it is not always the case that "purely domestic" is good.

Intellectual training and faith are necessary
To receive spiritual messages

There may well be some among our believers who have already developed a spiritual disposition through attending seminars in various places such as shojas [temples], and participating in ritual prayers. The other day, when I gave a lecture at Yokohama Shoshinkan, one of our facilities for religious training, there was a question during the Q&A session from somebody who claimed he was receiving inspiration from aliens and that he had become aware of the principle behind UFOs.

I took what was being said seriously at the time, but when I had our scientists listen to what that person had to say, it turned out that he did not seem to have attained that level of understanding. He seems to have thought that UFOs worked on the same principle as a spinning top, so he did not seem to have a complete understanding of it.

When it comes to receiving such ideas from other dimensions, you cannot verify their authenticity unless you have attained a certain level of knowledge in this world. You therefore have to be careful sometimes if you think that you are receiving many spiritual messages even though you have not yet reached a certain level. In such cases there is the possibility that you have been swallowed up by "another world," so discernment is very important here.

In that sense, it is important to train properly so that your ability to process things in real life does not decline when phenomena such as coming up with spiritual ideas, receiving revelations and seeing things in dreams start to occur. Check to see whether or not you are making any mistakes in everyday matters in real life. If you have started making mistakes when processing reality, you need to be a bit careful. If spiritual phenomena have too much influence, you will find yourself doing many things that are psychologically odd.

Therefore, the more spiritual you become, the more you need to check whether you are processing things in the mundane world properly. It is safer if you also study worldly things as much as possible, for this will form the basis of those checks.

I am recommending that people study languages such as English to keep their mind sharp even in old age, but it is not only for that purpose. It is extremely important to do such intellectual training diligently on a daily basis, to avoid spiritual messages from strange sources. It is important, after all, to maintain a state where even viewed objectively, you are training your brain.

Having said this, however, you also have to be careful about this since in many cases people who train their brain too much will generally be the types who have no sense of the spiritual, and become atheists and materialists. Therefore it is important not to neglect the cultivation of this kind of wide-ranging intellectual base, while at the same time having faith and holding to your position of never forgetting to believe in a mighty power. It is important to have faith in order to dedicate yourself to this mighty power and unite with it while also continuing steadily with your habitual worldly efforts.

Keep firing "shells" with positive thinking

As well as the points I have just mentioned, basically it is important to "Be Positive." If you want to enrich your ideas, it is no good starting off with the attitude "I can't do it." Basically, it is important to acquire the habit of thinking about how you can get things done.

It is important to have a mindset of thinking positively, of thinking of how you can somehow achieve your goal, instead of having the reactive habit of quickly saying, "No, it is not possible." If you think that you have a strong tendency to be negative, you need to deliberately make an effort to change this attitude.

Ideas will not arise if you are negative. There will be a blockage of ideas, so you need to think about things positively. Please think in an affirming way, and consider positively and constructively whether there is something useful that you can do.

Sometimes these positive ideas can be crushed. They can sometimes be rejected and crushed by other people, but it is important not to give up easily. After all, it is important to keep on tackling things with a positive mindset.

If you keep on firing "shells," sooner or later they will hit home. You may not hit the target with the first shot, but you have to keep on firing again and again with a strong determination of never failing to hit your target. Go as far as shooting down your negative thoughts. You must not give up too easily. As it says on the cover of our book in the Laws series for 2014, *The Laws of Perseverance*, it is important to have the attitude: "Never give up."

Swiftly forget the negative experience of being shot down, change your mindset, and get back on your feet as quickly as you can with the resolve to try once more. A path opens up and good ideas come thick and fast to those who are able to do this.

Chapter Five

Resourceful Leadership

~ Requirements for a Leader
Who Can Motivate Others ~

Lecture given on January 26, 2014
at Yokohama Shoshinkan
Kanagawa, Japan

1
The Definition of a Leader in Various Situations

The meaning of "resourcefulness" in Modern society

This chapter deals with the somewhat difficult theme of resourceful leadership. As there is probably a diverse readership for this book, it is difficult for me to find points common to all on this subject. Nevertheless I aim to make it useful for people in any occupation or position.

Let me start by explaining the title. First, there is a word "resourceful." The 2014 NHK [Japan Broadcasting Corporation] historical drama centered around Kanbei Kuroda [1546 – 1604], a brilliant strategist during Japan's Warring States period, and those who know about him may find the word "resourceful" fairly easy to understand. However, we are not in the Warring States period now, so his way of carrying out his stratagems with wisdom cannot be applied straightforwardly in our society. When your life is at stake and you are dealing with life or death situations, it is a very serious matter.

The original Japanese word for "resourcefulness," *chibo*, means devising a stratagem using wisdom. In modern-day society the "wisdom" part of it can probably be understood fairly well. However, people today will find the "stratagem" part rather hard to accept fully if it means aiming to excel in a plot to annihilate the enemy or inflict a crushing defeat.

To some extent, wisdom is of course necessary. It is a question of whether you can construct a logical approach or a plan from among the various alternatives and combinations of ideas to achieve unexpectedly effective results, or attain your goal. In other words, it is a way of producing effective results using wisdom.

A leader is someone who knows *What he or she has to do*

The title of this chapter also uses the word "leadership" along with "resourceful." I have previously given a lecture called, *Leader No Joken* [Requirements to Be a Leader] which has also been made into a book [Published by Happy Science, only for participants in the seminar on that lecture. Available only in Japanese]. In it I said, "A leader is someone who knows what he or she has to do," and "Someone who does not know what he has to do unless he is given instructions by someone else does not qualify as a leader. Such a person is a follower and is suited to being a subordinate." In other words, a leader is someone who knows what work he needs to do now, without anyone telling him.

Of course, people other than company presidents, such as heads of division, will receive some form of orientation and instruction about the company's policies. They will certainly be given overall direction or taught the industry's general trends, but leaders are those who know what they must do in their position, wherever they are placed.

Furthermore, a leader is someone who, if he has people working under him, has a grasp of which parts of his work can be delegated to subordinates so that he can achieve a higher level of results himself.

There are different levels of leadership, from the very top to middle- and lower-level, but basically a leader is someone who knows what work he or she needs to do without being told.

What kind of person is a resourceful leader?

In the case of a large company, many people may work without anyone below them until they reach middle age. But regardless of whether he has subordinates or not, a leader is the type of person who is capable of deciding for him- or herself which tasks he or she must do.

To give an example from the military, there are no privates [the lowest ranking soldier] amongst jet pilots in the air force. They all have at least the ranking of a commissioned officer. After all, they are flying very expensive aircraft which cost billions of yen each, and they have to decide when to fight and when to flee, at the risk of their lives. There may be times when someone else is in the plane with them, but in any case, it is part of their job to come up with their own plan, which represents an important strategy. This cannot be left to someone who becomes paralyzed in battle without detailed instructions about what to do.

Thus, someone who cannot think like a leader is not suited to a position where, even though he may not have subordinates, he is given something rather valuable and entrusted with the freedom to fight as he sees fit.

Basically this leads to the definition of a leader as someone who is "expensive." Please do not forget this definition.

In terms of resourceful leadership, a resourceful leader is someone who constantly hones his wisdom, gathers various kinds of knowledge and information, and through practice has mastered this, transforming it into wisdom. He is also someone who, whilst acquiring something similar to enlightenment as a business owner or businessman, can produce an answer when asked what work he should do in his current situation.

The risks for organizations that employ managers Incapable of making decisions

In reality, there are many people whose job title is management but in fact all they do is keep their seat warm and drink tea. This is the case not only in small companies but in big ones too. There are also cases where people are no longer given tasks to do in their last year or so before retirement; they have already been cast aside and are just sitting waiting for retirement.

There are also probably many managers whose subordinates effectively do their work for them, and they themselves cannot give instructions, make decisions or express their opinions to their own bosses. In other words, these are people who in actuality have been shunted aside. People like this who cannot see what work they should do are no longer leaders; they have become what are known as lame ducks or goners.

Companies that have many such people in their management are at risk. These people hang on to their management positions simply because they are getting on in years, have many years of experience or have been with the company for a long time. But companies employing many of these people who cannot actually make decisions for themselves and do nothing without orders from the top are at a very dangerous stage, both in the present and for the future.

The bigger an organization gets, the harder it becomes to keep an eye on things. When you have only one or two subordinates, it is easy to know what work they are doing, but when you have subordinates working on different things in a variety of locations it is impossible to issue instructions individually. So, although it may be the job of the person at the top to make decisions about such things as overall policies, orientation and performance, it is the work of the leader entrusted with an area of responsibility to think about his area of jurisdiction and decide on the actions to be taken.

Someone who cannot do that will unfortunately be regarded as a burden. Such leadership is not necessarily proportionate to a person's age, nor is it connected to gender.

Furthermore, though there may seem to be differences in brainpower based on people's academic record when they were young, after they have been working for ten years or so, they enter a world where one's academic record becomes irrelevant. After ten years' experience, people will be judged by what they have learned, for example, what they have put into practice and the results they have achieved, so they enter a world where academic records alone matter less and less.

An ideal leader from the point of view of subordinates

Conversely, seen from the vantage point of a follower or subordinate, a leader is someone who knows what work needs to be done and issues directives, and also the person who provides an accurate assessment of the results the follower produces in the work he or she has been given by that leader.

For example, a leader is the person who tells you whether you did a good or bad job, and if you did a bad job, tells you what was bad about it, what should be done and where to improve it. Or, if you did a good job, he or she can make comments and offer opinions such as, "You worked hard on this bit, even harder than we expected. This is what you did but it was this bit here that we were hoping for as a company. Still, from an overall perspective, you deserve a positive assessment, or perhaps just a little short of that. So next time, you should try doing this." Someone who can do this has the qualities of a leader.

On the other hand, the kind of boss who knows nothing about it but simply sits at his desk will lead the company itself into a harsh "winter." So the more talented the person at the top, the better the company.

2
An Organizational Culture That Nurtures Leaders

Increase the number of people who can make Decisions within the organization

Having said this, there are limits to the brainpower of one person. So even though there may be plenty of people who can make accurate decisions within the limits of what they can see, it is no easy matter to get a clear view of the overall picture when it comes to work that remains unclear, that can only be seen indirectly or can only be understood from other people's reports. For this reason it is best to have as many "heads" as possible.

Of course, it is not desirable to have the situation where "too many cooks spoil the broth," or where everyone's opinions differ so wildly that nothing gets done. Although the overall policies must certainly be followed, people who, while following the overall policies, can use their own brainpower to think everything through when it comes to the work they have been assigned with, are trustworthy.

This is the same for religious work and other Non Profit Organization [NPO] style work, as well as corporate work. It would be very tough if delegating a task was at the level of issuing detailed instructions and saying, "Please do everything according to the manual." If a task is entrusted to someone, it is important that, to a certain extent, he should be able to grasp the situation, think carefully and understand for himself what needs to be done.

That is an ability required from those among a company's permanent employees who are expected to become management staff in the future. Still, a company that has managed to create an organizational culture where ordinary employees gradually become capable of making the kind of decisions required of management, and where part-time and temporary staff can also do so, will invariably achieve great results.

The high level of human resource training Seen in Starbucks part-timers

I am going to explain further by using a coffee shop as an example. Many members of the Happy Science Student Division work part-time at Starbucks, a chain of coffee shops that is very popular nowadays. So I often run into them in shops in various locations [*laughs*].

The coffee sold on the bullet trains, on the other hand, does not taste very good at all, to be perfectly honest. I did use to drink it but have not done so for ages now.

Nowadays I often buy coffee outside and take it onto the train with me. That is because the coffee sold in coffee shops tastes better than the coffee sold on the train.

Even if the coffee on the train were complimentary, I would still buy prior to boarding and take it onto the train. This is because it is better to drink good coffee than bad, even if I have to pay for it. The coffee on trains does not sell well so it gradually oxidizes and loses its flavor; things like this are a common occurrence.

The Starbucks that I mentioned earlier is extremely popular, and someone told me something very interesting about the employees there. Even if a part-timer is working as little as two days a week, he will notice a regular customer coming in at the same time of day. Upon spotting the customer, even the part-timer will start to make his coffee before the customer gives his order. This is because he never says anything other than "the usual." When he happens to get an employee who does not know him and gets asked, "What is the usual?" he gets really furious.

Certainly, to the customer there is no difference between a part-timer and a full-timer. He is buying coffee from Starbucks, so he probably finds it intolerable to be offered anything other than the service and quality he expects of Starbucks coffee. He always comes at the same time and drinks the same coffee, so the staff should understand what he means by, "The usual."

Moreover, he is cheerful and acts approvingly if the employee has started to prepare his coffee before he orders it and hands it over to him quickly, but if he is asked to clarify his order, he gets angry. That is what is expected not just of full-timers but of part-timers as well, so it demonstrates the level of the shop.

For this reason, it seems that when you are job-hunting, you can win a few points depending on where you have worked as a part-timer.

Strengthen the organization through Human resource training and boost profitability

Starbucks has various kinds of coffee, as well as tea, and apparently there is a manual on how to prepare them. But I was rather surprised to hear that there is no customer service manual. They have a manual with recipes but no manual dealing with customer service. This means that they are creating an intangible corporate culture.

In effect, Starbucks trains part-timers, who are non-regular employees, to function in the same way as regular employees. As far as I can see from published statistics, Starbucks is now making the highest profits among the food service industries that have entered the Japanese market with foreign capital.

So, if lower-level employees can gradually make decisions on matters that were essentially to be decided by upper management or executives, the organization will be strengthened, able to expand, and increase its profitability. Increasing profitability actually means that it can become a franchise retail establishment. A company cannot open chain stores unless it makes a profit, and this is the difficult part of expanding a company.

3
The Resourcefulness and Efforts Required to Establish Yourself As a Professional

Without profit there is zero potential for growth

In terms of profit, Happy Science is a non-profit religious corporation, so of course we do not carry out our activities with the aim of making a profit. However, as it is functioning within the principles governing this world, it is only natural that the issue arises of whether we can generate what in a company would be called profits.

Just like an ordinary company, without having the equivalent of "profits," we cannot open new branch offices, construct new shoshinkans [shojas or temples], build schools, open branch offices overseas or employ people. The scale of our activities would be limited if the profits and losses stayed even. When our equivalent of "expenses" is subtracted from our equivalent of "sales and income," if there were no portion equivalent to "profit," there would be zero potential for our future growth.

If our costs were simply covered by loans from a bank, we would be burdened with liabilities and there would then be the danger of bankruptcy. The situation is exactly the same for both religious corporations and companies.

Let me now focus on this term "profit." It is now roughly 33 years since I started on this work, and we are in our 28th year since we actually acquired the official status of a religion and opened our offices. During this time I have had to learn rather a lot about money.

For example, although it may be OK to do NPO-style work for free, I have really come to understand that work done for free can be surprisingly bad. In other words, if you consider that nothing comes cheaper than free, you do not have to take any responsibility, or check and reflect on whether you are meeting the customer's needs. You become irresponsible when you think, "It's free so it doesn't matter," and you no longer feel the urge to make the other party happy, or to inspire them, or to make them feel that they have learned something.

The costs of my lectures rose
As the size of the venue increased

Take, for example, my lectures. Initially, we generally held lectures in places such as community centers, so the cost of the venue itself was small as we could rent such places for around 100,000 yen. That meant that we only had to charge entrance fees of around 1,000 yen.

However, as we gradually used bigger venues capable of holding thousands or tens of thousands of people, the rental fees also increased and we were paying tens of millions of yen for a venue, including the set-up costs.

Now that we have built our own temples, we incur practically no expenses for holding lectures but when we did not have our own venue we needed to create various conditions to do so. In just one day, a podium needed to be constructed, seating prepared, lighting set up and so on. So, in addition to the rental fee, these costs all added up to quite a lot.

When we did a light show lasting just two or three minutes in places like the Yokohama Arena, we were charged around 10 million yen for the lighting alone since it was controlled by advanced computer technology. For our part, though, we did not know whether the play of lights in the show was really worth 10 million yen. It is impossible for someone who has never worked in that industry to judge that. You might be able to get some sort of an idea if other companies gave quotes of the price they would do it for. You could compare the quotes and the end results and see which would be better value. But if there were no such comparisons, the only thing to do would be to ask one company to do it.

Though I did think, "10 million yen is a lot of money for such a short time," when I was told that it was very difficult to get the lights to move automatically using computers, I felt that was probably true. I thought that we could hold a lecture without the light show, but I also felt that maybe it would create a good atmosphere. In any case, it gradually cost us a lot to hold seminars at outside venues.

As a professional,
I felt the pressure of taking money

Tickets for my lectures, which initially were 1,000 yen started to get more expensive: first they became 2,000 yen, then 3,000 yen, then 5,000 yen and eventually 10,000 yen. And depending on the seats, tickets could be 20,000 yen, 30,000 yen or 50,000 yen.

As the price goes up so does the pressure on me. It is only natural to shoulder a heavier burden when you have to offer something worthy of that price. Of course the events have to be successful; failure is not an option. And there is always the possibility that we will end up in the red if we are not careful.

Incidentally, there was an article in a weekly magazine in the past saying that we spent 6 billion yen on a lecture in Tokyo Dome but it was a total fabrication. The truth is that it cost us around 200 million yen, which included renting the venue, set-up fees and all the other expenses.

You cannot continue doing lectures at Tokyo Dome unless you sell related items and make even a slim profit from one lecture. Furthermore, once you have held big events, you gradually become unable to hold small ones. Whether or not we could continue doing such events, factoring in all that, was a very tough decision.

When I established myself as a professional in that way, the fact that I was taking money put me under a lot of pressure. To be perfectly honest, it was easy when the lecture tickets cost 1,000 yen. If tickets were still 1,000 yen now, I would be taking off my jacket and giving the lecture while fanning myself, saying, "Hopefully this is about your 1,000 yen's worth?" [*laughs*]. However, when tickets cost tens of thousands of yen, you feel quite a heavy burden.

Daily study is essential for a professional

So, what should you do if you want to become a professional? Of course, daily study is important. You have to build up your studies of various subjects by creating habits, and at the same time those who have a specific area of work need to study that subject as well. This is one example of "resourcefulness," and it is extremely important to study well.

If you are cutting corners while doing this, it becomes easily apparent. For example, people from all over Japan attended the lecture, which was transcribed to become this chapter. Cutting corners would have resulted in people no longer coming to my lectures. I know that they would not come unless we really implored them to. However, as long as I continue making efforts without cutting corners, many people will keep coming to my lectures, even from far away.

It often happens that people from distant places are selected during the Q&A sessions at my lectures in Tokyo Shoshinkan. I really admire them when I think about the fact that the traveling expenses for those who have come from places like Hokkaido, Kyushu or the Chugoku region may well be higher than the cost of the lecture. And I am constantly asking myself whether, in my work, I have provided them with something that makes it worth their while during the time I have been allotted.

I watch my lectures again on DVD afterwards to review them and check that the content was appropriate and correct. In this way I have the habit of self-reflection, and the pressure can be "heavy."

However, this can be applied to everything. To receive money for work is a serious matter.

The more the added value created by employees,
The bigger a company will grow

When it comes to professional work, there is a difference between permanent and casual employees. A company expresses its intention to support permanent employees throughout their working life unless they do something dishonest or are extremely slovenly in their work. This is why it is so hard to become a permanent employee.

Moreover, for a permanent employee it is not the natural right that comes with age to be given a position such as supervisor, chief clerk, section manager or general manager. Rather, even if a permanent employee is given a position, as the company becomes a public institution, he or she must be able to produce added value to be deserving of that position, otherwise that worker will become a burden for the company.

Basically, it is a question of whether the value of your work increases or not. If you are working alone, this will be evident from the assessments and backing you receive from clients, and if you have subordinates working under you it will be the achievements of the team as a whole.

So how does the value of an individual's work increase?

First of all, the bare minimum requirement is that things improve by your being positioned there, and that it is better with you there than without you. Someone whose very presence is a "minus" really is a hopeless case, and is only there to solve the problem of unemployment. In other words, if a company accepts such a person, it helps the country. You could even say that one reason companies are public institutions is that they provide relief work for the unemployed.

In any case, we can say that the greater the total added value you produce, the bigger your company will grow.

4

The Ability to Analyze Information Required of a Leader

Strategies and tactics vary according to The leader's judgment

When it comes to the strategies and tactics that a leader should choose, a form of competition comes into play. For example, many of the people studying in Happy Science management seminars actually run companies. They listen to the same seminar but what they get from it varies according to the individual.

One person was impressed by the strategy of concentration and focused his line-up on products that sell well, successfully lowering prices by buying in bulk and making a profit by selling lots of items, since they were cheaper than anywhere else. There is a company like this run by one of our members.

Meanwhile, the company of another member chose not to diversify but rather to guarantee a really strong line-up of a particular kind of product so people know that if they go there, they will find what they want. For example, there is one place that has an incredible line-up of curries.

Thus, people adopt different ideas from my lectures and use them in their corporate strategy. I expect that there still is plenty of scope for ingenuity here.

The ability to discern what is right
Amongst information that is publicly available

With regard to "Abenomics," I can see both factors that will probably bring about success and factors that will probably bring about failure. Therefore I have stated, "You must embark on management strategies suited to a time of perseverance. This will be a considerable test of endurance. The government may be taking the lead, but whether the economy will actually change is rather a thorny question" [refer to Ryuho Okawa *Management Strategy in the Age of Perseverance* (Tokyo: Happy Science, 2014)].

There is certainly an overall rise in Japanese share prices, and overseas investors are now making investments, but many Japanese investors are considering selling off. A lot of them intend to buy shares in small quantities and sell them off when the prices go up to make a profit, and there are not many who think that the economy itself is on the upswing. They still have a wait-and-see attitude.

Any professional economist has to consider whether the economic boom really can be sustained even when the consumption tax is raised twice. This may or may not be a success. The government will most likely control various data as it promotes the raising of taxes, so we must judge accurately what part of that information is true and what is being manipulated.

What someone in a managerial position, or someone entrusted to make those types of decisions, is able to discern from publicly available information becomes very important.

For example, according to the statistics in 2010, the Chinese GDP [Gross Domestic Product] overtook that of Japan. Three years later in 2013 it was announced that China's GDP was double that of Japan. I am sure that undoubtedly came as a big surprise to Prime Minister Abe. I can well understand the reason for his wanting to visit countries all over the world.

As I have stated, even if the government instructs the Bank of Japan to increase the money supply and tells the people of Japan to spend more money, that alone is not going to work since everyone is wary about the future. They will be in trouble if the "bubble" economy is again set to burst so it is not that easy to circulate money. People would borrow lots of money if the bank would lend it to them without any collateral, and if it was fine not to pay it back. However, it is tough to be told things later like "Pay it back since the value of the collateral has dropped."

I had forecast that overseas investment would increase and, just as I predicted, the prime minister has been going on overseas business trips and lending lots of money at practically no interest via international yen loans. Since they will ultimately be written off if repayment becomes impossible, they are a really good thing for the borrower countries. In fact, quite a few of these loans have been written off in the past.

However, whether these countries have been grateful for that aid remains uncertain. China alone has received around 6 trillion yen in ODA [Official Development Assistance] from Japan, but there is the possibility that this money was used not to build roads and bridges but for military spending, which puts Japan in a very dangerous position.

In any case, how to analyze publicly available information is a crucial matter of judgment.

China's intentions can be picked up Even from newspaper articles

Speaking of the doubling of China's GDP, there was an article in yesterday's newspaper [January 25, 2014] about crude steel production. To make it easier to understand, we can take this to be iron and steel, and if we look at iron and steel production in 2013, China has produced seven times more than Japan. Their iron and steel production is seven times greater, even though their GDP is only double that of Japan, so there is something odd here.

Examples of how they would use seven times the amount of iron and steel would be in building tremendously tall condominiums that need steel reinforcing bars and steel frames, or making cars. Another use would be for ships. However, just looking at the ratio of 7:1, I get the impression that they are intending to build ships as part of their maritime strategy.

Before a war, countries start to boost their iron and steel production, and they also need raw materials such as coke to melt iron ore. In this respect, we have seen China deploying diplomacy to obtain resources over the past few years and busily buying up resources in places such as Australia, Argentina, Brazil and Africa. When China started to buy land in an effort to gain control of iron ore, Australia finally said no and changed its tactics. Just by looking at such facts, it is immediately obvious that China seems to be preparing for something.

In this way, you have to check for anomalies, even in publicly available information, and figure out what the other party is thinking.

The company president also needs to restart His studies if English is going to be The in-house official language

In terms of business, you also need to analyze things such as the strategies of other companies in the same industry as you. You have to analyze whether or not their ideas are on target.

For example, there are companies that implement policies such as making English their official in-house language and are promoting the use of English because they truly think that they have to use English to strengthen their overseas strategy. However, there is also the possibility that some companies make English the official in-house language in order to reduce the differences in the criteria for hiring foreigners and Japanese. In this way they are trying to lower production costs by hiring more foreigners, since production costs will decrease if they manufacture their products overseas.

In other words, the management objective could be simply to lower wages under the pretext that the amount of production in Japan is not particularly high despite the high wages, whilst the amount of production overseas has increased so much, even though salaries there are low. This too is something that needs to be looked at closely.

While there can be various approaches to management, there is an increase in the risk of doing business in certain countries [country risk]*, such as the risk in China and the risk in Korea. Our government is starting to launch a policy to increase interaction with the Islamic world from now on. There may be some difficulties due to differences in culture and customs, but the government is now trying to increase the number of countries where people do not need visas to come to Japan, and basically it can be assumed that English will be used as the official language.

The Islamic world currently has a population of around 1.6 billion and this will probably increase to over 2 billion. And there are already many places where work can be conducted in English. Furthermore, there are around 1.2 billion people in India as well, so if we look at places where English is understood, we can see that there are at least 3 or 4 billion people who can work in the English-speaking world.

Taking that into consideration, it is reasonable enough for companies that aim to do business with foreign countries to appeal to employees within their company to make efforts with their English. Even though that may not be all-important, we cannot say that there is no risk in making a living solely in Japan.

---

* "Country risk" is the risk of losing profits when investing in or trading with another country, due to a change in their political, economic, or social environment, irrespective of the risk to an individual business.

If push comes to shove, doing business in English is one method of business expansion, and it is also an approach being backed by the state. Thus, although I know that you company owners are exceedingly busy with your work, you should probably tighten the "screws" and brace yourself to return to your English studies.

Of course, it would be rather tough if the president had to be the best at English in a company; that would be no easy goal to achieve. Still, employees are observing their president's attitude fairly and objectively. They will be impressed and feel, "He is making tremendous efforts for a person of his age," or "Where on earth does he find the time to study when he is so busy, has such a tough job, often goes on business trips and has meetings with various people?" Therefore, although the president does not necessarily have to be the most competent at English, in most cases people will follow a boss who does not make excuses like "I have no time," "I am busy with work" or "I am in bad health" and instead plugs away as best he can to hone skills that will serve as weapons.

5
The Wisdom Needed to Expand Business

Requirements for motivating people:
1) Establish a noble purpose

If you want to manage many people, there are at least two conditions that must be fulfilled. The first condition, which applies whether it is a national project, a private scheme or some other kind of project, is to have a noble purpose. Unless there is some aspect that is the equivalent of a noble purpose, ultimately many people will not follow you.

If we consider the Meiji Restoration in Japan in the 19th century, it immediately becomes clear what it means to have a noble purpose. Victory and defeat in the Meiji Restoration were effectively decided by whether the leaders were able to put forward a noble purpose.

For example, at the Battle of Toba-Fushimi the loyalist army numbered only four or five thousand men, while the shogunate forces had around fifteen thousand men. It is therefore clear that the shogunate forces would have won in a straightforward fight. However, even though the loyalist forces numbered merely four or five thousand men, they fought for the emperor under the Imperial banner and demonstrated that the shogunate was an enemy of the state. When they put forward this noble purpose, the shogunate forces went into full retreat.

Establishing a noble purpose is extremely important, and can enable an army of four or five thousand to overthrow an army of ten thousand. When the shogunate forces were regarded as the rebel army, their will to fight naturally drained away. It is unbearable to be labelled a rebel or traitor and when this is the case, the opponents can often win if they attack using this opportunity as momentum.

While this sort of noble purpose is often found in the sphere of politics or revolutions, it is also necessary for companies as well. This is true even when a company is still small, and the bigger it grows, the more important it is to have a noble purpose.

Put simply, a company needs to consider their noble purpose, how their growth, the sales of their products and the fact that more people choose their services over those of other companies can be of service to the people and prosperity of the country, as well as to the world. People who cannot think like that can only be said to be working as individuals. It is important to have a noble purpose if you want to utilize people to further expand a business entity. And you must not invent lies or fabrications regarding this. You have to think about an actual, genuine noble purpose.

In the age of the Three Kingdoms in ancient China, for example, Liu Bei Xuande was proud of being a descendant of the Han dynasty and vowed to restore it. Cao Cao, on the other hand, was ridiculed as "the grandson of a eunuch." But he also continued to fight for the noble purpose of restoring the Han dynasty, at least up until the time he became prime minister, though the Han dynasty ultimately disappeared.

Some kind of noble purpose is thus required to mobilize many followers, and the same holds true for companies as well.

Of course, Happy Science also sets out many noble objectives. Many people are strengthened by believing in the noble purpose we state and repeatedly emphasize. As a result, they find justice in fighting and winning. In that sense, whatever your work may be, it is important that it has a noble purpose.

Requirements for motivating people: 2) Being humble and having The attitude of Making an effort

Another condition is required of people who manage others. There are all kinds of leaders, from minor leaders like section chiefs and heads of division to top leaders like presidents. These leaders all need to have a noble purpose and, at the same time, as they grow as leaders they need to restrain their ego and remain humble from the perspective of others. It is extremely important to demonstrate an attitude of doing your very best for those around you and for many others without being two-faced.

Therefore, the higher the position you attain, the more you must acknowledge your own shortcomings, think about where you have to put in more effort and where you have to be more humble, and continue to make constant efforts even without being told to do so.

As I said earlier, a leader is someone who knows what work he has to do without being given instructions, and the higher the position a person attains, the more important it is that he or she maintains a humble attitude and continues to make unseen efforts. In other words, a leader should not be content to take things easy while many others work, or to delegate jobs to make things easy for themselves; they have to think about how to utilize the freedom they have gained.

In some cases, they may have more time, for example. Or perhaps they may also have more financial freedom. How do they utilize it then? How do they make time and money go round again and again, to increase them even further? What investments are they making to do that? Are they investing time and money? Are they making continual efforts while making good use of even the smallest amount of time available? Many people are actually really observing such things.

How to create employees like you
And train management staff

Many executives used their precious time on a Sunday to come and learn from this lecture on "Resourceful Leadership." Their employees may have been impressed by that. However, there is also the possibility that their leader was napping during the lecture. You must therefore prove that you did not nod off.

Of course, that does not mean that you should repeat the entire contents of the lecture at length to your employees. You can explain briefly what you learned from the lecture by talking about it in the morning meeting or distributing a summary. You have to make efforts in this way to increase the number of employees who are like you, or those who will become management staff.

Just now I used Cao Cao as an example, and he is also connected with *The Art of War*. *The Art of War* is a vaunted Chinese classic, although we do not know much about the author, Sun Tzu, who is mentioned only in Sima Qian's *Records of the Grand Historian*. Cao Cao, who lived in the age of the Three Kingdoms, annotated *The*

Art of War and the Cao Cao version of *The Art of War* [*The Annotation of Sun Tzu's Strategies*] was extant, so it is said to have been the basic text for the current version.

It is considered that if Cao Cao's annotations were removed, the remaining parts are what were written by Sun Tzu. Cao Cao, the man who was constantly engaged in military campaigns added brief explanations and annotations to *The Art of War*. This was because there are parts of this "art" that are ambiguous. For example, in *The Art of War* it says to "concentrate your forces" and also says "you should be like water" but it is hard to reconcile these two teachings.

"Concentrate your forces" means, for example, keep pushing forward in a united front, following the same formula which, simply put, can be taken as meaning "take on your competitors with your company's strongest product." This can also apply when it comes to the investment of personnel, material objects and money.

Meanwhile, "be as free as water and create your military formations and tactics in accordance with your enemy's movements" can mean to develop different kinds of products, produce various kinds of services, and make it impossible to guess what you will do next. Thus both ways are possible, and it is very difficult to know how to interpret this.

In that sense, what was admirable about Cao Cao was that he did not simply study and use *The Art of War* for his own sake, but also made an annotated version and had many copies transcribed, which he had his generals and staff officers, as well as potential future officers, read and study. In other words, he created a textbook, which he got his top staff to study so that he could train them to think the same way as he did. This is a very important approach.

The reason why Happy Science makes it a priority To solidify "software" into text

Happy Science also has the same attitude, and we are apt to prioritize solidifying our "software" in the form of teaching materials. Doing this enables us to teach and tutor other people so that we can increase the number of people who think like us. That is why we are emphasizing the importance of solidifying our teachings in text form.

For example, as we are establishing the Happy Science University [HSU], before its opening we have been making public the content of the lessons. This is something never seen or heard of before, anywhere.

Moreover, we are boldly publishing books that reveal what we will be doing at HSU. In other words, by putting our "software" into textbooks, we are making it a priority to create teaching materials [refer to publications such as Ryuho Okawa, *The New Idea of a University* (New York: IRH Press, 2014)].

Of course, there is a strong likelihood that the contents of our textbooks will be copied but as an issue, it will come down to the extent of the imitators' creativity.

In any case, you cannot expand a business unless you increase the number of people who share your way of thinking. Please consider this point carefully.

6
The Ability to Take Responsibility: An Essential Quality for a Leader

In this chapter I described a leader as someone who knows what work he or she has to do without being told by other people. And, having gone beyond this definition, I have also discussed the subject a little more deeply, and stated that a leader needs to have a noble purpose. I have also said that as your business expands, you need to minimize the "I." Do not waste your time but instead exert your ingenuity and creativity, and display an attitude of making an effort. You also need to acquire the ability to analyze data in a unique and discerning manner.

In today's society resourceful leadership is based upon continual study and the ability to discern things that other people have not noticed or have not yet thought about. If you are to fulfill your mission as a leader based on these attitudes, you need to have both decisiveness and the ability to get things done. These factors will be crucial.

And finally, a leader must also have courage. The outcome of your work will eventually become evident, but the type of person who avoids work that brings about clear outcomes is ultimately not suited to be a leader. Someone who is unable to take responsibility should remain a staff officer, however intelligent or knowledgeable he or she may be.

A person who has the capacity to be a general may be required to take responsibility for defeat. Since there may be defeats as well as victories, a leader must have sufficient courage to accept that, as well as taking responsibility whilst demonstrating good judgment, decisiveness and the ability to get things done. That does, of course, also include the courage to order retreat when necessary. I believe that is the stature of a leader.

To sum up, in order to become a leader you need to have the kind of stratagem that a staff officer possesses, and this must be accompanied by courage, decisiveness, the ability to get things done and the ability to take responsibility. This concludes this chapter in which I have talked in various ways about resourceful leadership.

Chapter Six

The Challenge of Wisdom

~ The Wisdom That Transcends Hatred
And Saves the World ~

Lecture given on December 14, 2013
at Makuhari Messe
Chiba, Japan

1

The Most Important Starting Point

The activities of Happy Science cover a wide range of fields and I myself have also been doing various kinds of work. Throughout this process, I have returned to the starting point many times and considered what is most important for human beings.

What is this "starting point"? In fact, it is something very simple and obvious, something that is quite easy to understand.

The contemporary world is a very complex and highly advanced society, and academics are specialized and divided up into small fields. Therefore, even if people have mastered their own specialty in a particular field, they have lost the higher perspective of simple truths, such as "What is a human being?" "Why are human beings born into this world?" or "Where do we come from, and where do we go to?"

Humans have become very knowledgeable in their separate subjects. There are more specialists now than anyone could ever have imagined one or two hundred years ago. They have a lot of confidence in their specialized fields of work.

However, when they are asked about their overall view of human life, for example, "What kind of being are you? What does it mean that you are a human?" very few of them are able to answer in a satisfactory way.

2
The True Meaning of The "Right to Know"

What human beings truly need to know

Currently, in Japan, there is much discussion about various subjects including the disclosure of information and the importance of the right to know. I agree that humans have a right to such knowledge. However, I want you to know that "the right to know" is not only about having the right to know what is happening in this world.

As a human, we really should know about who we truly are, and why we exist right now.

Why were we born and why are we alive now,
having this appearance, these abilities, talents, and roles?
Why do we experience joy, sorrow, and pain?
Why do we strive to live with kindness?
Why is it that we cannot help but continue making an effort, even if we wish to stop?
Why do we aim to improve ourselves, striving to progress a step or two further in an effort to achieve a higher spiritual level than where we are now?

If humans were thrown into this world by chance,
why are there people here who are determined
to give love to others?
Why are there those who try to give love to a great
number of people?

These are the fundamental questions for humans.

The more you expand your "right to know," the
more you will come to understand that conflict and
hatred prevail in many places around the world.

There is a group of people shining brilliantly In the midst of conflict and hatred

In the midst of these conflicts and hatreds, there is a
group of people who shine a brilliant light. They are
trying to overcome hatred while in the midst of it. They
are trying to transcend, to go way beyond conflict even
while they are in it. Every single day, they ceaselessly
make the utmost effort to push humankind even one
step forward.

Those who gather at Happy Science, too, are
continually doing what must be done within the
framework of their capabilities, little though it may be.
Our work is still very small compared to the population
of billions in the world. People around the world,

in over a hundred countries, are now listening to my lectures, but my voice is still not reaching far enough.

Every day, I give lectures or record the voices from other dimensions, and those are compiled into books to be published all over the world. However, they do not yet reach all people. This is very sad.

People today who are moving away from faith yield To a materialistic civilization

There is another way to look at the situation. When I give a lecture in Japan now, it is broadcast to different places all around the country via satellite. And, with the support of some media channels, some of my lectures are shown on TV as well.

In Africa, on the other hand, more than thirty million people have already seen my lectures on TV. There are those who listen to my lectures every week. There is such a difference between Japan and Africa, and this has to do with our attitude towards religion.

Why is it that the more industries develop, and the more advanced and materialistic a civilization becomes, the more people distance themselves from faith? This may be because you have imprinted in you the idea that faith is something that goes against this modern civilization or against this current age. Or perhaps it is because something inside of you would be ashamed if others found out that you believe in God or Buddha?

If this is the case, it means that in the face of the question, "From where are humans born into this world and why do we have life right now?" you are being defeated by the materialistic civilization on earth. Please be always mindful of this truth.

Academic studies need the brighter light of wisdom

Right now, we are starting a big movement to establish the Happy Science University [HSU].

In this era, various subjects of study are being taught at numerous universities. Knowledge gained through these academic studies becomes our education, and provides people with intellectual power or the power to think. This power serves to promote the advancement of the world, even if only a little, making the world more convenient. I am not denying the importance of this education.

In this world there are many poor countries, whose people are experiencing starvation from a lack of food, who are without shelter, who are without sufficient drinking water, who cannot protect the health of their families. There are countries that cannot even build badly needed infrastructure, such as roads or bridges.

It is very important to offer new knowledge and more advanced wisdom to people in those countries, to bring them salvation while still living in this world, and to help them prosper through the power of academic study.

Nevertheless, academics today need to attain a higher level. They need the light of wisdom.

The power of wisdom distinguishes knowledge
That makes people happy from that which does not

It comes down to: "For what purpose are you learning? For what purpose are you trying to gain knowledge? For what reason have you become knowledgeable and earned the respect of others now as a specialist?"

Those who earn the respect of many through the amount of knowledge they possess need to be aware that their opinions can either save a lot of people or lead them astray.

Knowledge itself is neutral. While knowledge appears to serve some purpose, in fact it can either harm people or make them happy.

Is the knowledge you have the kind of knowledge that makes people happy? Or is it the kind that harms people, and that will bring them suffering or sorrow in the end? What distinguishes this difference is the power of wisdom.

3
In This Earthly World, Give Others A Glimpse of Angelic Qualities

Attain wisdom that can save people,
Transcending the differences
And discrimination of this world

Then, how can we attain such wisdom? There is certainly no doubt that it can be attained through various daily studies and experiences. It is also true that by learning the precious teachings of your predecessors, you can gain a higher level of awareness and lead your life without making wrong decisions, and so become able to guide other people. But there is something more I want to say to you.

The reason why people are allowed to live in this world is very plain and simple. You are allowed to be born into this world for a simple reason. Human beings are like travelers who go back and forth between the two worlds: the Real World known as the other world, and the Earthly World known as this world.

While people live in this world, they forget about the world that they came from and become interested only in worldly matters. However, in the midst of these earthly lives, some people are able to find the power of virtue in the true world known as the Real World, the power that is necessary for people to live, and they embody it. These people are able to see this world as infinitely close to the Truth, that this world was created by God or Buddha.

If people look at this world with a worldly, discriminatory perspective, they will start differentiating or even discriminating against people because of their skin color, salary, social status, education, or place of birth. But if you look at the world from a higher perspective, the perspective of the spiritual world, you will find that such differentiation or discrimination is meaningless.

Rather, those very people who are disadvantaged in some way in a worldly sense, who are in harsher situations than the average person, who, in a midst of a painful struggle, are giving the best of themselves while trying to extend a hand of salvation to others, are actually the light of this world. They are the love of this world, the forgiveness of this world.

Despite the great difficulty of living in this world, if you are able to give others a glimpse of the qualities of angels, it means that you have gained wisdom, no matter how little it may be.

How to lead the people of your country
To happiness within a diversity of lifestyles

Currently the world is divided into about two hundred countries. While we all live in the same 21st century, countless people are living in completely different environments, under various guiding principles, policies of education, and political systems. As long as humankind is diverse, there will be many experiments in civilization and numerous ways of living. We cannot help but accept this fact.

However, when it comes to how to lead the people of your country to happiness, as long as the goal and purpose are clear, you can help them advance in the direction of the same mountain peak, although the methods and paths may be different.

Even after having taken into account such differences in methods and means, there are some people who cling to the methods that would spread unhappiness in society and around the world. It is also the role of Happy Science to provide a light, like the warm rays of the sun in spring, to shine on the stubborn hearts of such people.

I wish to spread the Truth quickly, far and wide

I am filled with the desire to spread the Truth quickly, swiftly, far and wide. However, in this actual world, our pace is as slow as that of a snail. We are barely, just barely inching forward.

From around 1990 I have been giving lectures in large halls that seat over ten thousand people. Of course, back then we did not have satellite broadcasts. The audience came to the venue every spring, summer, fall, and winter, to listen directly to my lectures.

Today, my lectures are being broadcast in over 3,500 places throughout Japan and around the world. Compared to earlier days, my teachings have spread much further.

However, our power is still not strong enough. Please be aware of this.

Victory in this world and the mission of El Cantare

With Japan as our home base we are now carrying out our activities to spread the Truth, but there are countries that regard Japan with hostility. It is only natural that there are different ways of thinking, and I believe it is valuable for each country to make efforts to mend the faults of other countries. It is true that Japan has not always been in the right.

However, I do believe that how the Japanese lived in the past should be judged on the basis of the results, that is to say, how Japanese are living today.

Some people express resentment toward Japanese people, saying that they will not forgive Japan for a thousand years. But if you practice the power of love and forgiveness even towards these people and wish for the happiness of all the people of the world, you can proclaim that you have already triumphed in this world.

If there are people who continue resenting Japanese people for another thousand years, so be it. We shall forgive them for two thousand years. If there are countries that claim Japan has done awful things to them for the past few hundred years, we shall continue to bring happiness to such countries for thousands and thousands of years.

Furthermore, hatred is born in this world because of differences in religion, for instance between Islam, Judaism, Christianity, Buddhism, and other philosophies and creeds. The mission of El Cantare is to eradicate such hatred.

Happy Science explains that El Cantare is the Being that has guided various world religions throughout history. From the perspective of the common thinking of people today, this statement may seem like a complete fantasy, pure imagination, an impossible idea, which would be rejected in today's academic world. From the perspective of what is accepted as "usual thinking" it will appear this way.

However, as Jesus taught, it is the fruits that show whether a tree is good or bad.

The work of the guiding spirits of Light on Earth

If the "fruits" that you bear are ones that overcome hatred and cause flowers of love to bloom all over the world, then the "tree," the origin of the teachings you learn, exists to save the world. This "tree" is called El Cantare.

Though people may call it something different, I am talking about the Origin, or the Only One. All religions, ideas, philosophies and the various academic studies of the world have branched off from this Original Source.

Today, philosophies have become so specialized and have divided into so many branches that their essence has been lost. Even if people explore religious studies, the essence of religion has been lost. Some who do research into Buddhist studies claim that the Buddha was a materialist or an atheist. There is even a country that respects Confucius but ignores spiritual things because Confucius did not teach about the other world. [According to a press report, at the Central Work Conference on Ethnic Affairs held in September 2014, China's president, Xi Jinping, stressed that Communist

Party members cannot follow any religion and that the party needs to maintain the principle that its members cannot practice religion.]

Just as sand covers everything over a long time, with the passage of time philosophies may become outdated and hidden. That is why, from time to time, the guiding spirits of Light descend to earth and right the delusions of people in this world. They correct people's mistakes or amend mistaken teachings to show us how the world should be, in a simple way. This is their work.

Historically, many such people met tragic deaths. There were many who were not understood by their contemporaries because they went against the usual thinking of the day or because their thinking was too far ahead of their time. There were many such people who came and fought, long before us.

4
Under the Banner of Imperishable Truth

Wisdom is to attain the Truth Universal to humanity

However, I dare say unto you.

>Life on earth is limited.
>But the Truth will never die.
>The Truth is imperishable.
>My words will live on for 500, 1000, 2000, 3000 years.
>They will definitely be etched into the history of humankind.
>By then, photographs and videos of El Cantare will be gone.
>There will most likely not be any left.
>However, it is a fact that a man was born in a small country in the Orient and, going out beyond Japan, taught the Gospel to all people of the world.
>Never allow this fact to be erased from the history of this world.

Please stop being satisfied merely by attaining the all-too-simple knowledge of this world. The reason that you are living in this world is to attain the universal Truth that transcends the knowledge of this world. That is what wisdom is.

From "the challenge of Entering the academic world" to "The challenge of wisdom"

We have already established two Happy Science Academies, a junior high and a high school, in the Eastern and Western regions of Japan. From 2015 onwards, we are planning to open HSU. We are taking on the challenge of entering the academic world as well.

Those who are regarded as "great scholars" in the academic world have been failing to fully convey their sincere gratitude and passionate love to the people of the world, and instead have become cold, selfish people who take love and respect from others. Seeing that this is the reality, I really wish to encourage people who have studied and are educated, to develop the capacity to love many. That "Challenge of Wisdom" is what I wanted to convey to you in this chapter.

From now on,
Grasp the Eternal Truth with your own hands.
Under the banner of Truth,
Let us fight till the very end
To create a Utopia on earth,
Not only for yourself alone,
But for the people around you,
For the people of your country,
And for the people of the world.

Afterword

With the development of technology, not only has there been an increase in the amount of information and knowledge that an individual or organization can possess, but also there have been dramatic improvements in terms of efficiency, or the time it takes to acquire them.

Modern people seem to be under the illusion that they are on the verge of becoming gods. Yet, on the other hand, it is hard to believe that people fiddling with their mobile phones or smartphones as they traverse a pedestrian crossing have become cleverer than Socrates or Kant.

In his speech at the 2014 entrance ceremony at the University of Tokyo, the Dean of the College of Arts and Sciences advised freshmen to halve the amount of time they spend on their smartphones and instead read books. It was a modern version of the warning given by a certain commentator in my era, "watching too much television will turn Japan into a country of hundred million idiots."

This book teaches how to lead a "classical" intellectual life in a modern context, as well as how to produce intellectual output. This is also a book on the theory of work, presented by an intellectual who transcends his times and somehow produces the highest output in the world.

Ryuho Okawa
Founder and CEO of the Happy Science Group
December 2014

ABOUT THE AUTHOR

Founder and CEO of Happy Science Group.

Ryuho Okawa was born on July 7th 1956, in Tokushima, Japan. After graduating from the University of Tokyo with a law degree, he joined a Tokyo-based trading house. While working at its New York headquarters, he studied international finance at the Graduate Center of the City University of New York. In 1981, he attained Great Enlightenment and became aware that he is El Cantare with a mission to bring salvation to all humankind.

In 1986, he established Happy Science. It now has members in over 165 countries across the world, with more than 700 branches and temples as well as 10,000 missionary houses around the world.

He has given over 3,450 lectures (of which more than 150 are in English) and published over 3,000 books (of which more than 600 are Spiritual Interview Series), and many are translated into 40 languages. Along with *The Laws of the Sun* and *The Laws Of Messiah*, many of the books have become best sellers or million sellers. To date, Happy Science has produced 25 movies. The original story and original concept were given by the Executive Producer Ryuho Okawa. He has also composed music and written lyrics of over 450 pieces.

Moreover, he is the Founder of Happy Science University and Happy Science Academy (Junior and Senior High School), Founder and President of the Happiness Realization Party, Founder and Honorary Headmaster of Happy Science Institute of Government and Management, Founder of IRH Press Co., Ltd., and the Chairperson of NEW STAR PRODUCTION Co., Ltd. and ARI Production Co., Ltd.

WHAT IS EL CANTARE?

El Cantare means "the Light of the Earth," and is the Supreme God of the Earth who has been guiding humankind since the beginning of Genesis. He is whom Jesus called Father and Muhammad called Allah, and is *Ame-no-Mioya-Gami*, Japanese Father God. Different parts of El Cantare's core consciousness have descended to Earth in the past, once as Alpha and another as Elohim. His branch spirits, such as Shakyamuni Buddha and Hermes, have descended to Earth many times and helped to flourish many civilizations. To unite various religions and to integrate various fields of study in order to build a new civilization on Earth, a part of the core consciousness has descended to Earth as Master Ryuho Okawa.

Alpha is a part of the core consciousness of El Cantare who descended to Earth around 330 million years ago. Alpha preached Earth's Truths to harmonize and unify Earth-born humans and space people who came from other planets.

Elohim is a part of El Cantare's core consciousness who descended to Earth around 150 million years ago. He gave wisdom, mainly on the differences of light and darkness, good and evil.

Ame-no-Mioya-Gami (Japanese Father God) is the Creator God and the Father God who appears in the ancient literature, *Hotsuma Tsutae*. It is believed that He descended on the foothills of Mt. Fuji about 30,000 years ago and built the Fuji dynasty, which is the root of the Japanese civilization. With justice as the central pillar, Ame-no-Mioya-Gami's teachings spread to ancient civilizations of other countries in the world.

Shakyamuni Buddha was born as a prince into the Shakya Clan in India around 2,600 years ago. When he was 29 years old, he renounced the world and sought enlightenment. He later attained Great Enlightenment and founded Buddhism.

Hermes is one of the 12 Olympian gods in Greek mythology, but the spiritual Truth is that he taught the teachings of love and progress around 4,300 years ago that became the origin of the current Western civilization. He is a hero that truly existed.

Ophealis was born in Greece around 6,500 years ago and was the leader who took an expedition to as far as Egypt. He is the God of miracles, prosperity, and arts, and is known as Osiris in the Egyptian mythology.

Rient Arl Croud was born as a king of the ancient Incan Empire around 7,000 years ago and taught about the mysteries of the mind. In the heavenly world, he is responsible for the interactions that take place between various planets.

Thoth was an almighty leader who built the golden age of the Atlantic civilization around 12,000 years ago. In the Egyptian mythology, he is known as god Thoth.

Ra Mu was a leader who built the golden age of the civilization of Mu around 17,000 years ago. As a religious leader and a politician, he ruled by uniting religion and politics.

ABOUT HAPPY SCIENCE

Happy Science is a global movement that empowers individuals to find purpose and spiritual happiness and to share that happiness with their families, societies, and the world. With more than 12 million members around the world, Happy Science aims to increase awareness of spiritual truths and expand our capacity for love, compassion, and joy so that together we can create the kind of world we all wish to live in.

Activities at Happy Science are based on the Principle of Happiness (Love, Wisdom, Self-Reflection, and Progress). This principle embraces worldwide philosophies and beliefs, transcending boundaries of culture and religions.

Love teaches us to give ourselves freely without expecting anything in return; it encompasses giving, nurturing, and forgiving.

Wisdom leads us to the insights of spiritual truths, and opens us to the true meaning of life and the will of God (the universe, the highest power, Buddha).

Self-Reflection brings a mindful, nonjudgmental lens to our thoughts and actions to help us find our truest selves—the essence of our souls—and deepen our connection to the highest power. It helps us attain a clean and peaceful mind and leads us to the right life path.

Progress emphasizes the positive, dynamic aspects of our spiritual growth—actions we can take to manifest and spread happiness around the world. It's a path that not only expands our soul growth, but also furthers the collective potential of the world we live in.

PROGRAMS AND EVENTS

The doors of Happy Science are open to all. We offer a variety of programs and events, including self-exploration and self-growth programs, spiritual seminars, meditation and contemplation sessions, study groups, and book events.

Our programs are designed to:
* Deepen your understanding of your purpose and meaning in life
* Improve your relationships and increase your capacity to love unconditionally
* Attain peace of mind, decrease anxiety and stress, and feel positive
* Gain deeper insights and a broader perspective on the world
* Learn how to overcome life's challenges
  ... and much more.

For more information, visit happy-science.org.

CONTACT INFORMATION

Happy Science is a worldwide organization with branches and temples around the globe. For a comprehensive list, visit the worldwide directory at *happy-science.org*. The following are some of the many Happy Science locations:

UNITED STATES AND CANADA

New York
79 Franklin St., New York, NY 10013, USA
Phone: 1-212-343-7972
Fax: 1-212-343-7973
Email: ny@happy-science.org
Website: happyscience-usa.org

New Jersey
66 Hudson St., #2R, Hoboken, NJ 07030, USA
Phone: 1-201-313-0127
Email: nj@happy-science.org
Website: happyscience-usa.org

Chicago
2300 Barrington Rd., Suite #400,
Hoffman Estates, IL 60169, USA
Phone: 1-630-937-3077
Email: chicago@happy-science.org
Website: happyscience-usa.org

Florida
5208 8th St., Zephyrhills, FL 33542, USA
Phone: 1-813-715-0000
Fax: 1-813-715-0010
Email: florida@happy-science.org
Website: happyscience-usa.org

Atlanta
1874 Piedmont Ave., NE Suite 360-C
Atlanta, GA 30324, USA
Phone: 1-404-892-7770
Email: atlanta@happy-science.org
Website: happyscience-usa.org

San Francisco
525 Clinton St.
Redwood City, CA 94062, USA
Phone & Fax: 1-650-363-2777
Email: sf@happy-science.org
Website: happyscience-usa.org

Los Angeles
1590 E. Del Mar Blvd., Pasadena, CA 91106, USA
Phone: 1-626-395-7775
Fax: 1-626-395-7776
Email: la@happy-science.org
Website: happyscience-usa.org

Orange County
16541 Gothard St. Suite 104
Huntington Beach, CA 92647
Phone: 1-714-659-1501
Email: oc@happy-science.org
Website: happyscience-usa.org

San Diego
7841 Balboa Ave. Suite #202
San Diego, CA 92111, USA
Phone: 1-626-395-7775
Fax: 1-626-395-7776
E-mail: sandiego@happy-science.org
Website: happyscience-usa.org

Hawaii
Phone: 1-808-591-9772
Fax: 1-808-591-9776
Email: hi@happy-science.org
Website: happyscience-usa.org

Kauai
3343 Kanakolu Street, Suite 5
Lihue, HI 96766, USA
Phone: 1-808-822-7007
Fax: 1-808-822-6007
Email: kauai-hi@happy-science.org
Website: happyscience-usa.org

Toronto
845 The Queensway
Etobicoke, ON M8Z 1N6, Canada
Phone: 1-416-901-3747
Email: toronto@happy-science.org
Website: happy-science.ca

Vancouver
#201-2607 East 49th Avenue,
Vancouver, BC, V5S 1J9, Canada
Phone: 1-604-437-7735
Fax: 1-604-437-7764
Email: vancouver@happy-science.org
Website: happy-science.ca

INTERNATIONAL

Tokyo
1-6-7 Togoshi, Shinagawa,
Tokyo, 142-0041, Japan
Phone: 81-3-6384-5770
Fax: 81-3-6384-5776
Email: tokyo@happy-science.org
Website: happy-science.org

Seoul
74, Sadang-ro 27-gil,
Dongjak-gu, Seoul, Korea
Phone: 82-2-3478-8777
Fax: 82-2-3478-9777
Email: korea@happy-science.org
Website: happyscience-korea.org

London
3 Margaret St.
London, W1W 8RE United Kingdom
Phone: 44-20-7323-9255
Fax: 44-20-7323-9344
Email: eu@happy-science.org
Website: www.happyscience-uk.org

Taipei
No. 89, Lane 155, Dunhua N. Road,
Songshan District, Taipei City 105, Taiwan
Phone: 886-2-2719-9377
Fax: 886-2-2719-5570
Email: taiwan@happy-science.org
Website: happyscience-tw.org

Sydney
516 Pacific Highway, Lane Cove North,
2066 NSW, Australia
Phone: 61-2-9411-2877
Fax: 61-2-9411-2822
Email: sydney@happy-science.org

Kuala Lumpur
No 22A, Block 2, Jalil Link Jalan Jalil
Jaya 2, Bukit Jalil 57000,
Kuala Lumpur, Malaysia
Phone: 60-3-8998-7877
Fax: 60-3-8998-7977
Email: malaysia@happy-science.org
Website: happyscience.org.my

Sao Paulo
Rua. Domingos de Morais 1154,
Vila Mariana, Sao Paulo SP
CEP 04010-100, Brazil
Phone: 55-11-5088-3800
Email: sp@happy-science.org
Website: happyscience.com.br

Kathmandu
Kathmandu Metropolitan City,
Ward No. 15, Ring Road, Kimdol,
Sitapaila Kathmandu, Nepal
Phone: 977-1-427-2931
Email: nepal@happy-science.org

Jundiai
Rua Congo, 447, Jd. Bonfiglioli
Jundiai-CEP, 13207-340, Brazil
Phone: 55-11-4587-5952
Email: jundiai@happy-science.org

Kampala
Plot 877 Rubaga Road, Kampala
P.O. Box 34130 Kampala, UGANDA
Phone: 256-79-4682-121
Email: uganda@happy-science.org

BOOKS BY RYUHO OKAWA

THE LAWS OF THE SUN
One Source, One Planet, One People

ISBN: 978-1-942125-43-3
$15.95 (Paperback)

IMAGINE IF YOU COULD ASK GOD why He created this world and what spiritual laws He used to shape us—and everything around us. If we could understand His designs and intentions, we could discover what our goals in life should be and whether our actions move us closer to those goals or farther away.

At a young age, a spiritual calling prompted Ryuho Okawa to outline what he innately understood to be universal truths for all humankind. In *The Laws of the Sun*, Okawa outlines these laws of the universe and provides a road map for living one's life with greater purpose and meaning.

In this powerful book, Ryuho Okawa reveals the transcendent nature of consciousness and the secrets of our multidimensional universe and our place in it. By understanding the different stages of love and following the Buddhist Eightfold Path, he believes we can speed up our eternal process of development. *The Laws of the Sun* shows the way to realize true happiness—a happiness that continues from this world through the other.

THE LAWS OF GREAT ENLIGHTENMENT
ALWAYS WALK WITH BUDDHA

ISBN: 978-1-942125-62-4
$17.95 (Paperback)

Buddhist Approaches to Become Stress-Free

In this modern society, people tend to live a stressful life and experience hurting others or being hurt by others. Often they find themselves unable to forgive someone, making it difficult for them to maintain a peaceful mind. However, there are ways to lead a stress-free life and enjoy happiness from within.

This book offers you the practical approaches to achieve it. By understanding the Buddhist concept "enlightenment" described here, you will gain the power to forgive sins and get to know how to be the master of your own mind, not a slave to your emotions.

After reading this book, your view of the world will completely change, and come to understand that we are living in a beautiful world that God created.

THE LAWS OF PERSEVERANCE
REVERSING YOUR COMMON SENSE

ISBN: 978-1-937673-56-7
$14.95 (Paperback)

"No matter how much you suffer, the Truth will gradually shine forth as you continue to endure hardships. Therefore, simply strengthen your mind and keep making constant efforts in times of endurance, however ordinary they may be.

Eventually, you will come out of your slump and overcome your hardships. And, as you try and aim to reverse the common sense, you will one day understand that people can be "undefeated" even if they seem to have lost in this world. In that process, you may sometimes feel that virtue is being generated."

—From Postscript

THE NINE DIMENSIONS
Unveiling the Laws of Eternity

ISBN: 978-0-9826985-6-3
$15.95 (Paperback)

THIS BOOK IS YOUR GATE TO HEAVEN. In this book, Master Okawa shows that God designed this world and the vast, wondrous world of our afterlife as a school with many levels through which our souls learn and grow. This book is a window into the mind of our loving God, who encourages us to grow into greater angels.

SECRETS OF
THE EVERLASTING TRUTHS
A New Paradigm for Living on Earth

ISBN: 978-1-937673-10-9

$14.95 (Paperback)

OUR BELIEF IN THE INVISIBLE IS OUR FUTURE. It is our knowledge about the everlasting spiritual laws and our belief in the invisible that will make it possible for us to solve the world's problems and bring our entire planet together. When you discover the secrets in this book, your view of yourself and the world will be changed dramatically and forever.

"To save the seven billion people on Earth,
God has countless angels working constantly,
every day, on His behalf." —Chapter 3

THE MOMENT OF TRUTH
BECOME A LIVING ANGEL TODAY

ISBN: 978-0-9826985-7-0
$14.95 (Paperback)

MASTER OKAWA shows that we are essentially spiritual beings and that our true and lasting happiness is not found within the material world but rather in acts of unconditional and selfless love toward the greater world. These pages reveal God's mind, His mercy, and His hope that many of us will become living angels that shine light onto this world.

CHANGE YOUR LIFE, CHANGE THE WORLD
A SPIRITUAL GUIDE TO LIVING NOW

ISBN: 978-0-9826985-0-1
$16.95 (Paperback)

MASTER RYUHO OKAWA calls out to people of all nations to remember their true spiritual roots and to build our planet into a united Earth of peace, prosperity, and happiness. With the spiritual wisdom contained in this book, each and every one of us can change our lives and change the world.

THINK BIG!
BE POSITIVE AND BE BRAVE TO ACHIEVE YOUR DREAMS!

ISBN: 978-1-942125-04-4

$12.95 (Paperback)

In *Think Big* Master Ryuho Okawa shares his own philosophy of thinking big, thinking positive, and being brave for they are essential mindsets in achieving our dreams. While there is an especial emphasis on developing this philosophy while we're young, it is universal and valuable for people of all ages and all walks of life who want to achieve their dreams and live a successful life. If you do not have any dreams yet, then this is a must-have book for discovering why having ideals are an essential part of life. If you already have aspirations, then discover how to make them come true. If you are in college, find out valuable tips on how to get a head start on developing the think big mindset.

ALSO BY RYUHO OKAWA

THE TEN PRINCIPLES FROM EL CANTARE VOLUME I
Ryuho Okawa's First Lectures on His Basic Teachings

THE TEN PRINCIPLES FROM EL CANTARE VOLUME II
Ryuho Okawa's First Lectures on His Wish to Save the World

THE GOLDEN LAWS
History through the Eyes of the Eternal Buddha

THE STARTING POINT OF HAPPINESS
An Inspiring Guide to Positive Living with Faith, Love, and Courage

LOVE, NURTURE, AND FORGIVE
A Handbook to Add a New Richness to Your Life

AN UNSHAKABLE MIND
How to Overcome Life's Difficulties

THE ORIGIN OF LOVE
On the Beauty of Compassion

INVINCIBLE THINKING
An Essential Guide for a Lifetime of Growth, Success, and Triumph

GUIDEPOSTS TO HAPPINESS
Prescriptions for a Wonderful Life

THE LAWS OF HAPPINESS
Love, Wisdom, Self-Reflection and Progress

TIPS TO FIND HAPPINESS
Creating a Harmonious Home for Your Spouse, Your Children, and Yourself

THE PHILOSOPHY OF PROGRESS
Higher Thinking for Developing Infinite Prosperity

THE ESSENCE OF BUDDHA
The Path to Enlightenment

THE CHALLENGE OF THE MIND
An Essential Guide to Buddha's Teachings:
Zen, Karma, and Enlightenment

THE MANIFESTO OF THE HAPPINESS
REALIZATION PARTY

RYUHO OKAWA: A POLITICAL REVOLUTIONARY
The Originator of Abenomics and Father of the Happiness Realization Party

SPIRITUAL MESSAGES FROM
THE GUARDIAN SPIRIT OF RYUHO OKAWA
The Divine Voice of Shakyamuni Buddha

THE IMPORTANCE OF
THE EXPLORATION OF THE RIGHT MIND

INTO THE STORM OF
INTERNATIONAL POLITICS
The New Standards of the World Order

HIGHER EDUCATION SERIES

THE NEW IDEA OF A UNIVERSITY
The Groundbreaking Mission of Happy Science University

THE BASIC TEACHINGS OF HAPPY SCIENCE
A Happiness Theory on Truth and Faith

IN LOVE WITH THE SUN
SPIRITUAL MESSAGES FROM GODDESS GAIA

Ryuho Okawa & Shio Okawa

ISBN: 978-1-941779-26-2
$14.95 (Paperback)

After 600 million years, people shall know the true genesis.

The true story when the earth was born, The guiding concept of the earth, The mechanism of creating life on Earth. And the future that human beings has to seek, These secrets are now revealed by the spiritual message from Goddess Gaia, Who supported the creation of Earth civilization by Alpha, the God of origin.

Through reading this book, you will see the magnificent scale of El Cantare's Law.

"I would like for you to listen to the bell ringing the advent of a spiritual revolution."

— Ryuho Okawa, Preface

THE TRUTH OF THE PACIFIC WAR
Soulful Messages from Hideki Tojo,
Japan's Wartime Leader

ISBN: 978-1-941779-22-4

$14.95 (Paperback)

In this book, we provide you with the material needed to rethink whether or not the perception of World War II by the winners was right, through looking back on history starting with the current world affairs. This is all necessary for us to get a thorough understanding of ongoing confusion in the world and to seek the path of peace, stability and progress of future humankind.

The material provided is a new testimony by General Hideki Tojo, who is enshrined at Yasukuni Shrine and who was Japan's most significant figure in the Pacific War. Furthermore, we have also recorded a testimony by Supreme Commander of the Allied Powers Douglas MacArthur in order to ensure a fair argument.

A NEW MESSAGE FROM VLADIMIR PUTIN
INTERVIEWING THE GUARDIAN SPIRIT OF THE PRESIDENT OF RUSSIA

ISBN: 978-1-937673-94-9

$14.95 (Paperback)

We hereby bring you the most recent spiritual message from the guardian spirit of President Putin, the politician who is the center of attention of not just the people of Russia but of the whole world, regardless of it being in a good or a bad way. In the Preface, it says, "President Putin's true intentions, which are 90 percent misunderstood."

We hope that, through this book, the reader will come to understand the true thoughts of Mr. Putin which are still undisclosed to the public. And, we hope that the reader will foresee the new world order that this skilled politician is thinking of, and make use of that in predicting how the international affairs will turn out in the future.

THE SECRET BEHIND
"THE RAPE OF NANKING"
A SPIRITUAL CONFESSION BY IRIS CHANG

ISBN: 978-1-941779-08-8
$9.95 (Paperback)

Sometimes a single book can determine how the international society sees history, as well as give a great impact on international relations. If a fabricated history had spread throughout the world and is subjecting the citizens of a particular country to humiliation that they don't deserve, then speaking from international justice and humanitarian viewpoints, such history must be rewritten in an objective and impartial manner. There is a phrase, "History is written by the victors." The usual process is that, after a war, the victors come up with a one-sided historical view that is advantageous to them and historical researchers of later generations gradually make corrections to it.

Nevertheless, sometimes history takes a sudden turn due to revelations from Heaven. This book is a rare example of that. The author of a book which gave a great impact on the historical view that had spread throughout the international society today confessed the truth regarding the content of her book and its background, just 10 years after her death, in a form of a spiritual message.

THE GENIUS OF ICHIRO
The Secret Behind His Four Thousand Hits

ISBN: 978-1-941779-04-0
$14.95 (Paperback)

Ichiro Suzuki arrived in Seattle in 2001 as a mostly anonymous free agent from Japan's NPB, and while there was buzz about his potential, no one really knew what to expect. Since then, he has set many records in American Major League Baseball, including the record for most hits in a single season (262) and longest streak of two-hundred-hit seasons (ten years). On August 21, 2013, he got the four thousandth hit of his professional baseball career. This spiritual interview reveals the "making of Ichiro," including the secrets to his professionalism, his techniques for overcoming slumps, and how he made it to the top. The interview highlights Ichiro's unique traits that continue to impress us, twelve years after he first unleashed the laser beam.

ON HAPPINESS REVOLUTION
A Spiritual Interview with Hannah Arendt

ISBN: 978-1-937673-82-6
$14.95 (Paperback)

Since 2010, Master Ryuho Okawa has published over two hundred spiritual messages, in Japanese, from the spirits of historical men and women and the guardian spirits of today's living figures. With this Spiritual Interview Series, Master Okawa is now making these important messages available in English. The books in this series are messages from the spirits or guardian spirits of people who have a great deal of influence over world affairs. These messages reveal these powerful figures' hidden intentions and disclose facts that even news reporters would have difficulty drawing out. Master Okawa's in-depth analyses of these messages give us the tools that we need to understand and confront the dangers that lie ahead of us. Master Okawa hopes to show readers that the spirit world and spirits are real, and that by understanding spiritual truths, we can bring a peaceful end to international conflicts and create solutions to a variety of global crises.

ARE ISLAMIC EXTREMISTS JIHADISTS OR TERRORISTS?
THE NECESSITY OF FREEDOM IN ISLAMIC COUNTRIES

ISBN: 978-1-941779-14-9

$14.95 (Paperback)

The West has been leading a long war on terror since the 9/11 terrorist attacks in 2001 on American soil by Osama bin Laden's al-Qaeda. Even after the assassination of Osama bin Laden on May 2, 2011, by President Obama's Special Forces unit, terrorist attacks have continued around the world. On January 16, 2013, an international crisis erupted when Islamic terrorists organized by Mokhtar Belmokhtar lay siege to an Algerian gas plant. After the Algerian government sent in a special forces unit, thirty-nine foreign hostages were killed and 685 Algerian workers and one hundred foreigners escaped or were freed.*

Are the attacks by Islamic extremist groups like al-Qaeda and the organization led by Mokhtar Belmokhtar unjust acts of terror? Or are they justified acts of a holy war, as the self-proclaimed jihadists claim? In this interview with Osama bin Laden, Master Ryuho Okawa provides us with his conclusive answer to these questions.

* "Q&A: Hostage Crisis in Algeria," BBC News, January 21, 2013, http://www.bbc.com/news/world-africa-21056884.

LEADERSHIP SECRETS OF LIU BANG
THE EMPEROR OF CHINA'S HAN DYNASTY
WITH A SURPRISING CONNECTION WITH STEVEN SPIELBERG

ISBN: 978-1-941779-17-0

$14.95 (Paperback)

Liu Bang, also known as Gaozu, began from humble peasant roots and served as a police officer under the Qin dynasty. He rose through the ranks, first receiving control of western China, and eventually becoming the ruler of China as the founder and first emperor of the Han dynasty (206 BCE–220 CE). The histories of kings and rulers often provide valuable lessons about the universal principles that can be applied to today's management, entrepreneurship, and all types of large undertakings. As this spiritual interview has shown, Liu Bang's strengths and achievements are marked by a strong global element. Everyone who aspires to lead a large organization can learn from his ability to win people's hearts. You may be surprised to discover that this long-ago emperor of China is living today in the United States as one of the world's most famous film directors, Steven Spielberg.

THE TRUTH OF NANKING AND COMFORT WOMEN ISSUES
A Spiritual Reading into World War II
by Edgar Cayce

ISBN: 978-1-937673-86-4

$14.95 (Paperback)

Did the so-called "Nanking Massacre" and the military comfort women forcefully taken by the Japanese troops actually exist as historical facts? In this book, we attempt to investigate whether the two events actually took place by using a new method. This is not merely to restore the international honor of Japan. We are hoping to review the causes of World War II, look over the world justice made by the victorious nations after the war and reveal the true world history.

THE NEW DIPLOMATIC STRATEGIES OF SIR WINSTON CHURCHILL
A Spiritual Interview with the Former Prime Minister Regarding the Age of Perseverance

ISBN: 978-1-937673-85-7
$14.95 (Paperback)

Today, two politicians are criticized and compared to Hitler; President Vladimir Putin of Russia and Prime Minister Shinzo Abe of Japan. Are these politicians really dangerous to be likened to Hitler? Or, just like in Hitler's case, can it be that another truly dangerous politician exists in another country that is yet to be discovered? If there is a chance to hear the opinion of Sir Winston Churchill, considered to be Hitler's arch enemy, journalists around the world would probably be interested to hear this.

The series on Spiritual Messages by Ryuho Okawa, Happy Science, made this possible. This book contains a record of an interview conducted with the spirit of former British Prime Minister Churchill by Master Okawa in March this year. It is a record of an interview on issues related to the "next appearance of Hitler," and on current international affairs.

THE ART OF BUSINESS REVITALIZATION
MANAGEMENT WISDOM FROM JACK WELCH, CARLOS GHOSN, AND BILL GATES

ISBN: 978-1-937673-70-3

$19.95 (Paperback)

In *The Art of Business Revitalization: Management Wisdom from Jack Welch*, Carlos Ghosn, and Bill Gates, Master Ryuho Okawa conducts spiritual interviews with three of the greatest executives of our time. General Electric's Jack Welch, Renault and Nissan's Carlos Ghosn, and Microsoft's Bill Gates give readers a glimpse into how they took hold of opportunities and turned them into successes. What management philosophies helped Jack Welch and Carlos Ghosn turn around their companies during downturns? What is Bill Gates's secret to creating products that become global standards? What human resources management and education philosophies have they drawn upon to keep their companies at the top? This book reveals the secrets to their achievements.

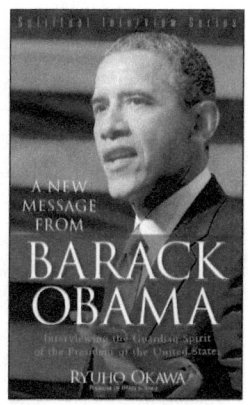

A NEW MESSAGE FROM BARACK OBAMA
INTERVIEWING THE GUARDIAN SPIRIT OF THE PRESIDENT OF THE UNITED STATES

ISBN: 978-1-937673-89-5
$14.95 (Paperback)

In April 2014, President Obama embarked on his fifth trip to Asia during his time in office to discuss the pressing issues in the Asia-pacific region. A week before his Asia trip, Master Ryuho Okawa held a spiritual interview with Barack Obama, which revealed his true objectives of his Asia tour and about his thoughts on current affairs in the world. What is President Obama's vision of America's role in the world today? Why does he believe that America is not the world's policeman? This spiritual interview reveals President Obama's stance on international relations including America's relationship with China, the Ukraine crisis and Islamic extremism. It also discloses his honest feelings about Japanese Prime Minister Abe and Russian President Putin. Now that America is "on the verge of crisis," as the guardian spirit of President Obama says in this interview, we all need to think about how we can achieve security, justice and peace in the world without the "world's policeman."

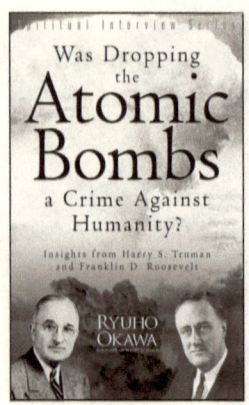

WAS DROPPING THE ATOMIC BOMBS
A CRIME AGAINST HUMANITY?
INSIGHTS FROM HARRY S. TRUMAN
AND FRANKLIN D. ROOSEVELT

ISBN: 978-1-937673-78-9

$14.95 (Paperback)

Was there any true justification for the atomic bombing of Hiroshima and Nagasaki? To answer to this question, Master Ryuho Okawa conducted spiritual interviews with Harry S. Truman and Franklin D. Roosevelt, the two presidents who presided over the United States' participation in World War II. Could anything justify the use of nuclear weapons on civilians? Was Pearl Harbor really a sneak attack, or did Franklin Roosevelt know of it beforehand? This book reveals valuable information that will help the world gain a truthful understanding of world history.

JAPAN! REGAIN YOUR
SAMURAI SPIRIT

A MESSAGE FROM THE GUARDIAN SPIRIT OF LEE TENG-HUI,
FORMER PRESIDENT OF THE REPUBLIC OF CHINA

IISBN: 978-1-937673-77-2
$14.95 (Paperback)

This book is the record of interviews conducted on Former President of
Taiwan Lee Teng-hui's subconscious [guardian spirit] in February 2014.
His true thoughts, as well as the truth on modern East-Asian history,
were revealed in these interviews. The book is filled with hints on how
to give another thought to the causes of World War II. As it is stated in
the afterword, this is a book which we want "all politicians, all people in
the media, and everyone who talks about politics" to read.

DIPLOMATIC STRATEGY
FOR JAPAN, U.S. AND CHINA
A MESSAGE FROM THE GUARDIAN SPIRIT OF
DIPLOMATIC ANALYST HISAHIKO OKAZAKI

ISBN: 978-1-937673-75-8

$14.95 (Paperback)

This book contains the interview conducted with the guardian spirit of former diplomat, Hisahiko Okazaki, a conservative commentator representative to Japan. An astonishing relation between Admiral Perry and Okazaki is revealed in this interview. By reading this book, you will come to know what Admiral Perry thinks on the current situation of the world, and the relation between Japan and the United States, 160 years later since he opened up Japan which was in seclusion.

WHY I AM ANTI-JAPAN
INTERVIEWING THE GUARDIAN SPIRIT OF
KOREAN PRESIDENT PARK GEUN-HYE

ISBN: 978-1-937673-67-3
$14.95 (Paperback)

This book is the record of interviews conducted on President Park's subconscious [guardian spirit] in February 2014, which were done in order to find out the fundamental reason to her anti-Japanese sentiments. Her true thoughts, as well as the truth on modern Japan-Korea history, were revealed in these interviews. By having numerous people in the world know of this truth, starting with the Japanese, South Koreans, Americans and the Chinese, the path to create a constructive future of the Pacific Basin should open as we resolve the conflicting emotions between Japan and South Korea in the international society.

A WARNING TO
SOUTH KOREA'S PRESIDENT
WORDS FROM HER FATHER,
FORMER PRESIDENT PARK CHUNG-HEE

ISBN: 978-1-937673-65-9

$14.95 (Paperback)

Park Chung-hee served as the president of the Republic of Korea (South Korea) for almost sixteen years, from 1963 until his death in 1979. Today, people around the world know him as the assassinated father of Park Geun-hye, the current and first female president of South Korea. In this spiritual interview, Park Chung-hee's spirit shares his opinions on the roles of South Korea, Japan, the United States, China, and North Korea in the global context. What are his thoughts on the Takeshima island dispute, the comfort-women issue, China's future prospects, and the direction South Korea should take as a country? A Warning to South Korea's President is a father's message to his daughter as he seeks to guide their nation in the right direction. This interview lets us see history in a new light and shows us how to build a better future for the Asia-Pacific region.

INTERVIEWING THE
GUARDIAN SPIRIT OF U.S. AMBASSADOR
CAROLINE KENNEDY
A NEW BRIDGE BETWEEN JAPAN AND THE U.S.

ISBN: 978-1-937673-63-5

$14.95 (Paperback)

CONTENTS

1 Caroline's Guardian Spirit Makes an "Informal" Appearance
2 Her View on Japan-U.S. and Japan-China Relations
3 True Emotions Behind America's Disappointment in Yasukuni Visit
4 World War II
5 Comfort Women Issue and Women's Rights
6 The Reason Behind the Kennedy Tragedies
7 Drive-Hunt Dolphin Killing, and Japanese vs. American Cultures
8 Japanese Princess and Roman Emperor in Past Lives?
9 Message to Japan

FOR THE FUTURE OF THAILAND AND JAPAN
INTERVIEWING THE GUARDIAN SPIRIT OF YINGLUCK SHINAWATRA

ISBN: 978-1-937673-59-8

$14.95 (Paperback)

In December 2013, Thailand's Prime Minister Yingluck announced the dissolution of the nation's parliament and called a snap election to be held in February 2014. But this did not appease the thousands of angry protestors who remained on the streets of Bangkok.

During this time of social unrest, Prime Minister Yingluck were mostly absent from Bangkok to avoid protestors, spending more time in the Northern and Northeastern areas. It was in such a difficult time for the prime minister and the country of Thailand that Master Ryuho Okawa conducted a spiritual interview with Prime Minister Yingluck. In this spiritual interview, the guardian spirit of Prime Minister Yingluck shares her views on many controversial topics including democracy in Thailand, Thailand's relationships with China and Japan, traditional Buddhism, and Islam. She then asks Japan to help her country which has plunged into turmoil. It is Master Ryuho Okawa's hope that this interview will become a bridge to build a wonderful relationship between Thailand and Japan.

MOTHER TERESA'S
CURRENT CALLING IN HEAVEN
THE SAINT OF THE GUTTERS DELIVERS HER EXPERIENCES OF
GOD, HEAVEN, AND OUR MISSION

ISBN: 978-1-937673-55-0

$14.95 (Paperback)

This book is a spiritual interview with Mother Teresa's spirit who talks through Master Ryuho Okawa. In this spiritual interview, which was conducted sixteen years after Mother Teresa's death, Mother Teresa's spirit talks about her astonishing discoveries about God, Heaven, and the mission that people on earth should aim to fulfill through life. Mother Teresa reveals that the other world is a vast place with many levels of angels, that Heaven and Hell exist, and that the reality of the human being is the soul. In addition to a discussion about the contradictions within Christian teachings and the need for new teachings for today's people, she also talks about her discoveries about God and Jesus Christ, and says that it is the mission of the wealthy to help others who are in poverty, through prayer and a pure heart.

NELSON MANDELA'S LAST MESSAGE
A Conversation with Madiba
Six Hours After His Death

ISBN: 978-1-937673-53-6
$14.95 (Paperback)

On December 5, 2013, the entire world mourned the passing of Nelson Mandela. Even as the news was spreading, Mandela's spirit came to Master Ryuho Okawa to give us all an important message of hope and to prove that the afterlife exists. Archbishop of Canterbury Justin Wilby paid this tribute to the first black president of South Africa and the man who liberated his country from apartheid: "His courage was undefeated, indomitable, extraordinary." Perhaps it was Mandela's indomitable belief in the fundamental reality of the human soul that gave him such extraordinary courage in the face of adversity. For as he says in this spiritual interview, God created our souls as thinking energy without color, and that our colorless soul is the basis of our fundamental freedom and equality. In this spiritual interview, Master Ryuho Okawa gives us a glimpse into the mind of this great leader whose undefeated spirit is a message of hope to us all.

SOUTH KOREA'S CONSPIRACY
PRESIDENT PARK'S HIDDEN AGENDA TO UNITE WITH CHINA

ISBN: 978-1-937673-51-2
$14.95 (Paperback)

On June 27, 2013, South Korea's President Park Geun-hye and Chinese President Xi Jinping held summit talks in Beijing. At the meeting, President Park asked China's Xi Jinping to build a memorial of An Jung-geun, the man who in 1909 assassinated the first Prime Minister of Japan and the first Resident-General of Korea, Ito Hirobumi. In this spiritual interview, we begin by speaking with the spirit of An Jung-geun before moving on to a conversation with the guardian spirit of President Park, who forced herself into the interview out of fear that the interview will reveal the truth about him. Through these conversations, Master Ryuho Okawa tries to discover the facts about the assassination of Ito Hirobumi to determine whether An Jung-geun can justifiably be hailed as a hero. While South Koreans continue to accuse Japan of having wronged their nation, Master Okawa hopes that these interviews will provide a truthful understanding of the historical events between Japan and South Korea and help the international community understand the nature of true international justice.

MARGARET THATCHER'S MIRACULOUS MESSAGE
AN INTERVIEW WITH THE IRON LADY
19 HOURS AFTER HER DEATH

ISBN: 978-1-937673-37-6

$14.95 (Paperback)

On April 9, 2013, just nineteen hours after Margaret Thatcher's death, Master Ryuho Okawa summoned her spirit to hold a miraculous spiritual interview with Europe's first female prime minister, famously known as the Iron Lady. In words marked by her signature clarity and determination, Margaret Thatcher provided valuable answers to essential and timely questions. Her answers will prove helpful not only to the United Kingdom, but also to the global economy and governments all over the world, including those of the United States and the European Union.

UNMASKING BAN KI-MOON'S BIASED STANCE
INVESTIGATING THE PARALYSIS OF THE UNITED NATIONS

ISBN: 978-1-937673-49-9

$14.95 (Paperback)

The world is currently facing many critical international issues that require resolution through strong leadership dedicated to the preservation of international peace and security. What are U.N. Secretary-General Ban Ki-moon's true thoughts on these pressing issues? What does he think about the disputes between Japan and South Korea over ownership of the Takeshima Islands, between Japan and China over ownership of the Senkaku Islands, and between Iran and Israel over nuclear weapons capability? Can we depend on him to successfully uphold the principle of impartiality in the United Nations's role of peacemaking? In this spiritual interview with the guardian spirit of Mr. Ban Ki-moon, Master Okawa reveals the U.N. Secretary-General's true character and true intentions regarding his important peacemaking responsibilities.

STEVE JOBS RETURNS WITH HIS SECRETS
BE SIMPLE, BE CRAZY

ISBN: 978-1-937673-47-5

$19.95 (Paperback)

In this spiritual interview with Steve Jobs, conducted just three months after his death, Master Okawa offers us a chance to catch a glimpse into the mind of one of America's modern geniuses, whom President Barack Obama has described as one among the greatest American innovators. What was the aesthetic philosophy behind his passionate drive to create products that he described as "at the intersection of art and technology?" What were the secrets to his creativity and the successful sales of his products? As Master Okawa often says, and as this interview with the mind of one of the greatest modern innovators will show you, success is always in the way we think and in the substance of our goals and ideals.

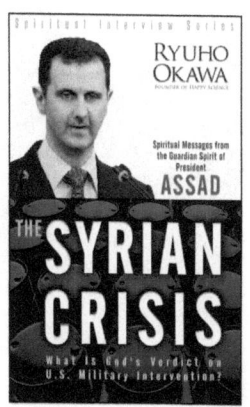

THE SYRIAN CRISIS
WHAT IS GOD'S VERDICT ON U.S. MILITARY INTERVENTION?

ISBN: 978-1-937673-44-4

$14.95 (Paperback)

Is there justice in a U.S. military intervention into the ongoing Syrian crisis? What is God's perspective on the tragedy that is occurring in Syria? In *The Syrian Crisis: What Is God's Verdict on U.S. Military Intervention?* Master Ryuho Okawa conducts a spiritual interview with the guardian spirit of Bashar al-Assad. As this interview reveals, the Syrian dictator's true character is quite different from what we saw in the CBS interview. As the world braces for a possible world war, Master Ryuho Okawa provides us with a clear sense of where God's justice lies in this international crisis.

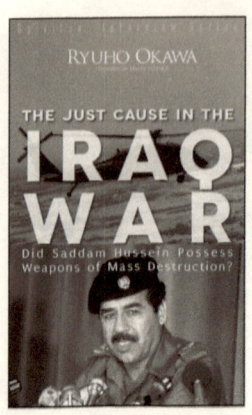

THE JUST CAUSE IN THE IRAQ WAR
Did Saddam Hussein Possess
Weapons of Mass Destruction?

ISBN: 978-1-937673-41-3
$14.95 (Paperback)

The Just Cause in the Iraq War: Did Saddam Hussein Possess Weapons of Mass Destruction? tackles one of the most controversial and pertinent issues in international politics today. Is President Obama correct that the Iraq War was an unjust war, as he claimed during the 2012 presidential race? Did Saddam Hussein truly have no weapons of mass destruction, or are those weapons still hidden in Iraq, somewhere beyond the reach of U.S. intelligence? In this book, you will discover that Saddam Hussein was also behind the planning of the 9/11 terrorist attacks and both he and Osama bin Laden are now in Hell. The knowledge this book provides will help each of us make the right decisions as we work together to create a peaceful international society.

FORECASTING THE SECOND KOREAN WAR
HOW WILL THE WORLD HANDLE THE CRISIS?

ISBN: 978-1-937673-35-2
$14.95 (Paperback)

Forecasting the Second Korean War: How Will the World Handle the Crisis? forecasts a potential crisis that the United States, South Korea, and Japan may face. In part 1, Master Okawa draws on the help of Edgar Cayce to describe in detail the unfolding of a second Korean War that could begin in the summer of 2013. Part 2 of this book contains a spiritual interview with Kim Il Sung that reveals that he is spiritually guiding Kim Jong Un. Together, the two parts of this book reveal the shocking fact that the crisis on the Korean peninsula is only a small part of a larger and more global imperialistic scheme that is being masterminded by Xi Jinping, the president of China. You will discover who is truly behind the Islamist terrorist attacks against the United States.

EXPOSING NORTH KOREA'S
MENACING LEADER
KIM JONG UN'S PLOT FOR A PSYCHOLOGICAL WAR

ISBN: 978-1-937673-39-0
$14.95 (Paperback)

Exposing North Korea's Menacing Leader: Kim Jong Un's Plot for a Psychological War reveals the role that North Korea is playing in China's imperialistic strategy and the two nations' close ties with Iran. Together, China and Kim Jong Un—North Korea's supreme leader—are carrying out a psychological war that takes full advantage of the weaknesses of Japanese Prime Minister Abe and United States President Obama. Indeed, this interview with Kim Jong Un's guardian spirit reveals that Kim Jong Un was most likely behind the Boston marathon bombings that occurred on April 15, 2013.

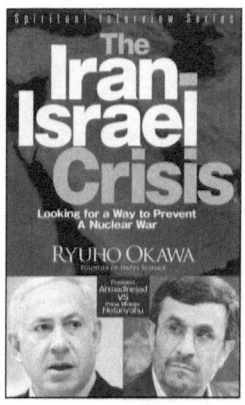

THE IRAN-ISRAEL CRISIS
LOOKING FOR A WAY TO PREVENT A NUCLEAR WAR

ISBN: 978-1-937673-26-0
$14.95 (Paperback)

Master Ryuho Okawa firmly believes that the power to create lasting global peace will come from embracing love and forgiveness beyond differences in religion. This set of spiritual interviews with the guardian spirits of Iran's President Mahmoud Ahmadinejad and Israel's Prime Minister Benjamin Netanyahu reveal their living counterparts' underlying ideas about each other's nations as arch enemies. You will discover hints to solving long-standing clashes between religions.

CHINA'S SECRET MILITARY BASES
A REMOTE-VIEWING INVESTIGATION
OF SUSPICIOUS SATELLITE IMAGES

ISBN: 978-1-937673-24-6

$14.95 (Paperback)

Master Okawa reveals China's versions of Area 51 from mysterious satellite photos that had aroused worldwide curiosity. Even American intelligence will be shocked to find out these truths about a hidden enormous missile-launching site full of nuclear warheads prepared to strike major cities around the world. This book is a must-read for anyone who wants to save the world from a full-out nuclear war.

HAVE FAITH IN GREAT AMERICA
LIBERTY AND WORLD JUSTICE FOR ALL

ISBN: 978-1-937673-20-8

$14.95 (Paperback)

Have Faith in Great America: Liberty and World Justice for All is Master Ryuho Okawa's earnest message to the United States of America. The world's future depends on America's fulfillment of its long-held sacred mission of protecting the faith, liberty, and justice of people and nations around the world, and on the development of strong bonds between the United States and Japan.

CHINA'S HIDDEN AGENDA
THE MASTERMIND BEHIND THE ANTI-AMERICAN
AND ANTI-JAPANESE PROTESTS

ISBN: 978-1937673-18-5

$14.95 (Paperback)

"Anti-American demonstrations have been raging in over twenty Arab countries. The man pulling the strings behind all this is Xi Jinping."

—Master Ryuho Okawa

"I wanted to stir up the anti-American movement in the Arab world to make sure that the United States won't be able to attack Syria or Iran...I'm the mastermind behind the Muhammad video."

—Xi Jinping's Guardian Spirit

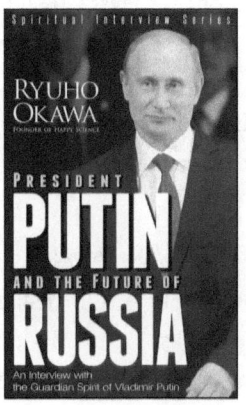

PRESIDENT PUTIN AND THE FUTURE OF RUSSIA
An Interview with the Guardian Spirit of Vladimir Putin

ISBN: 978-1-937673-14-7

$14.95 (Paperback)

"I have no intention of fighting the United States. The Cold War is over... I have no intention of fighting the Americans... And I'm not friendly enough with China to think about joining them against the United States... I have given Russians religious freedom, which makes me very different from the Chinese."

—Putin's Guardian Spirit

ABOUT HS PRESS

HS Press is an imprint of IRH Press Co., Ltd. IRH Press Co., Ltd., based in Tokyo, was founded in 1987 as a publishing division of Happy Science. IRH Press publishes religious and spiritual books, journals, magazines and also operates broadcast and film production enterprises. For more information, visit *okawabooks.com*.

Follow us on:

f Facebook: Okawa Books   Instagram: OkawaBooks
▶ Youtube: Okawa Books   Twitter: Okawa Books
P Pinterest: Okawa Books   **g** Goodreads: Ryuho Okawa

――――――― **NEWSLETTER** ―――――――

To receive book related news, promotions and events, please subscribe to our newsletter below.

∞ eepurl.com/bsMeJj

 ――― **AUDIO / VISUAL MEDIA** ―――

YOUTUBE   **PODCAST**

Introduction of Ryuho Okawa's titles; topics ranging from self-help, current affairs, spirituality, religion, and the universe.